100 ACTS

OF MINOR DISSENT

MARK THOMAS

sept
em
b
er

1 3 5 7 9 10 8 6 4 2

First published in 2015 by September Publishing

Copyright © Mark Thomas 2015

Cover art, book design and illustrations by Greg Matthews
www.designbygreg.uk

Printed in China on paper from responsibly managed,
sustainable sources by Everbest Printing Co Ltd

ISBN 978-1910463031

www.markthomasinfo.co.uk
www.septemberpublishing.org
Tell us what you think @SeptemberBooks

PROLOGUE

'WHERE DO YOU GET YOUR IDEAS FROM?'

When you are as famous as I am, you have to do a lot of interviews with local newspapers to sell tickets for your gigs. So the question, 'Where do you get your ideas from?' is oft heard. Here are some of the answers I have given.

'A stall in Brick Lane. They literally sell random ideas in plastic bags; it's a tenner a bag. You never know what you are going to get in them, and sometimes I end up phoning Andy Parsons, saying, "Look I've got a bag of ideas, I can't use this stuff but you might be interested."'

'I have a team of drunken dwarves who write ideas in marker pen on my naked body.'

'Pixies.'

'I paint pictures with my breakfast and start with the first image I see emerge from the yolk.'

'Ikea.'

'I watch *Family Guy* repeats on BBC3 until my mind wanders off to somewhere interesting.'

'It was 2 a.m. in a hotel on Saddleworth Moor while my agent shouted "I'm not leaving the room until you tell me what the new show is about!"'

The last one is true.*

2 a.m. – 7 March 2013 in a hotel room on Saddleworth Moor, my agent and I hold a late-night creative workshop. Sitting amid matching rose-patterned wallpaper and pillow cases, squeezing plastic milk teat sachets into cups of tea, while the wind on the moor rattles the windows, this is our cultural world; Dostoevsky meets Alan Bennett.

The idea of doing a show called '100 Acts of Minor Dissent' had been floating around for a while, but I had always put it off. Perhaps because to commit the 100 and tour a show around the country performing for

---

* As is the breakfast one.

two hours for 200 nights of the year is hard work. Perhaps because I thought a better idea might come along. Perhaps because a better idea had come along.

At 2 a.m. my agent screws up his face and says, 'I am not leaving this hotel room until you tell me what the new show is about.'

I blurt out the idea. He shouts, 'Great!' Five minutes later he has left the room. Nine hours later he tells me the first gigs have been booked and I am committed to carrying out 100 Acts of Minor Dissent in the course of a year.

'Where do you get your ideas from?'

I get them from the panic induced by my agent squatting my hotel room and shouting at me.

'So why are you doing this?'

I really do a lot of interviews with local newspapers, so many I can lip-synch the follow-up question, ***'Aren't you getting too old for all of this?'*** Let me take the questions one at a time.

An Act of Dissent is a simple way of saying, 'No, I do not accept this and, as my silence may be construed as acquiescence, I would like to make a small gesture to indicate that you can all go fuck yourselves.' It is the rebuttal of the thin end of the wedge. It is a way of saying no to the countless small compromises we make each day.

Look, I say to the local arts correspondents, I live in the same area my family has lived in for generations, my sister is vicar in the local church, my cousins used to live at the end of the street, my nan and granddad were air raid wardens in WW2 and their shelter used to stand just one minute's walk from where I live now. Here they are on their fire truck.

I love the fact that my children went to the same primary school I went to.

I love that their head teacher used to teach me.

I love feeling part of my community.

I love that my old postie and I swap biographies on punk and new wave musicians.

I love that when I go into my local independent coffee shop they say one word, 'Espresso?' And when my wife isn't with me they say, 'Cake?'

I like the fact that Terry the tramp doesn't beg off of locals when he is pissed.

I like that we buy him coffee when he is sober.

I love that when walking past my local barber sporting a cut from another establishment he came out into the street and in a shocked voice bellowed, 'Oi, you seeing another barber?' then walked back inside loudly proclaiming to anyone who would listen, 'It's as if he wanted to be caught.'

I love where I have been born and raised, but where there was once a hospital at the end of the street there is now a Tesco, literally. The old cinema is a wine warehouse; the local deli run by the mad Italian guy who made up the prices according to what mood he was in, that's gone. We have a Tesco, a Costa, Sainsbury's Local, another Tesco and estate agents: loads of estate agents; a rash of arrogant Mini Cooper-driving Dapper Laughs wannabes.

So I am doing 100 Acts of Minor Dissent because I love local communities and the way they work, and I hate the way neoliberalism turns our streets into bland replicating copies of each other. And, yes, I am aware I sound like a Marxist Victor Meldrew but, guess what, I'm over 50 and I don't give a fuck.

———————◆———————

TWO STORIES ON THE NATURE OF DISSENT

When my son was four years old I took him and his grandmother to Tate Britain *(Tate Ancient)*. I said, 'Today, son, we are going to an art gallery.'

He innocently responded, 'Will any of my pictures be there?'

He had no idea that to be on display in a 'proper' art gallery you had to qualify as an artist and be approved by a series of critics and curators. For him, art was something you did and then put on the wall. Not wishing to crush youthful aspiration, I replied in neutral tones, 'Not unless we take some up.'

'Can we?' he said.

'Yes,' I replied.

'I'll find the Blu-Tack,' he said helpfully.

So we set off to the Tate, my son and I, accompanied by my mother-in-law *(she's a devout Catholic, a volunteer at Oxfam and reads the* Daily Mail*; I feel compelled to say that I love her)*. We casually walked in with my son's paintings rolled in my hand, wandered around for a while and shortly found a quiet spot near a series of oil paintings, then deftly hung my son's works in their rightful place.

I recently found the video footage I took of that event. My son stands in a yellow Pokémon fleece next to his drawing of a spider and says to me, 'Will anyone buy them, Dad?'

'We'll have to see,' I say.

Then my mother-in-law interjects, 'Well they're a lot better than most of the stuff in here.'

Looking back on that event there are two clear categories of dissenter in this story: my son, the accidental dissenter, and my mother-in-law, who knew you are not supposed to hang your own pictures in an art gallery, the transgressor. I see my role in this story as mentor.

These are not fixed roles; as my son got older his role changed from innocent to transgressor.

He came home from school aged 16 in a rather truculent state.

'What's up?'

'I'm in trouble with English.'

'Why?'

'I was a minute late and the teacher shouted at me, "You are a minute late for an English lesson – that is disgusting."'

'What did you reply to the teacher?' I enquired.

'I said … "It's not disgusting, miss … it is tardy. It is regretful, it could be rude, it could display a belligerent or ambivalent attitude towards the class, but it is not disgusting, and as we are in an English lesson I think we should use the appropriate word."'

Some are born dissenting, some achieve dissension and some have dissent thrust upon them.

———————◆———————

ACTS 1-10

BOOKS, BARBIE CARS & BREEZE BLOCKS

AND SO IT BEGINS ...

ACT 1 The Legal Deposit Libraries Act 2003 requires a publisher to deposit two copies of every book with the British Library; it is a nice law and has existed in some form in the UK since 1662. It means every book ever published since that date is held in perpetuity by the library, forming a cultural and intellectual archive for the nation.

I found this out in 2013, after self-publishing the play script of *Bravo Figaro!*, a play I had written about my dad.

I do not react well to legal letters unless I am sending them. So when the British Library legal deposit team wrote me a legal letter, a somewhat threatening letter, saying, 'Unless you send two copies of *Bravo Figaro!* to the legal deposit library within 14 days of receipt of this letter we will fuck you up with paper cuts from the index cards!'* I behaved to type and the following day I sent the British Library a box of 100 copies of *Bravo Figaro!* with a note:

Dear British Library,

RE: Donations compliance.

These have not been selling as well as I had hoped and are looking for a good home. If anyone wants to take a copy out of the library you might actually give them their own personal copy. Perhaps charge a small admin fee, say £5 and then, if you wouldn't mind, send the money to me.

Bless them, they replied.

---

* Strictly speaking this quote is inaccurate, but that was the legal gist.

> Dear Mark,
>
> Many thanks for the box with copies of your book *Bravo Figaro!* and the accompanying note. Sorry to hear this isn't selling so well.
>
> Unfortunately our bookshop isn't geared up for the kind of arrangement you suggest.
>
> We'd like to send copies to the other five legal deposit libraries and to approach READ International (which supports literacy in Africa).
>
> *All the best.*

Frankly, if everyone replied with the same grace and wit as the British Library I would be out of a job.

Fortunately, the target of ACT 2 reacted with the dignity and charm of a masturbating clown.

I assembled a few friends to help with this Act: my long-term collaborator Tracey Moberly *(artist from the Welsh Valleys)*, Dr Bipasha Ahmed *(neighbour and psychology lecturer)* and fellow comic Josie Long.

I presented these intelligent, incisive and creative women with the most appropriate and meaningful gift I could find – a remote-control Barbie car. A bright and stunning pink toy with the words 'Beautiful Girl' on the bonnet.

'Why do this?' you ask.

'Because I am a feminist,' I reply.

One morning we took the cars up to Mayfair and then my friends raced them outside the Saudi Arabian Embassy.

The time trials outside the embassy gates resulted in a definitive winner:

1st *SAUDI ARABIAN EMBASSY*
WOMEN'S CAR RACE

1st	**Dr Bipasha Ahmed**	*12.30 seconds*
2nd	**Tracey Moberly**	*18.04 seconds*
3rd	**Josie Long**	*23.00 seconds*

While we were taking the victor's photo, some of the diplomatic staff from the embassy ran up to the railings, shouting and furiously jabbing their fingers in the air. 'If you let them drive, THEY KILL THEIR CHILDREN!'

The Barbie cars are currently on loan to transsexual and transgender activists who will be racing them outside the Russian Embassy.

———————◆———————

ACT 3 is a variant on a popular Act of Dissent, namely this: the epitome of good manners in all decent homes is, upon receipt of junk mail containing a Freepost pre-addressed envelope, to a) insert the contents of the junk mail into the prepaid envelope, and b) post it back to the fuckers that sent it. This is based on the sound logic that if someone sends you their rubbish you are entitled to send it back, at their expense.

My variation on the practised etiquette on receipt of unwanted missives is based on the idea that if someone sends me rubbish I am entitled to send it back AND some of my own.

Foxtons estate agent sent me a glossy card inviting me to sell my home; I sent back Weetabix. This was accompanied with a note that the company should regard this as a request to be removed from their mailing list.

A motor company sent me half a tree's worth of promotional cack; I sent back an out-of-date tin of sardines.

Things took a turn for the weird when I received a note from the postman explaining a letter addressed to me did not have the correct postage on it and if I wished to receive the letter I should go to the post office, pay a small fine and the value of the postage. Which I did. The letter was a leaflet from Will's Art Warehouse.

Enraged at paying for a promotional leaflet, I inserted a large unwanted hardback book into a Jiffy bag and posted it to Will's Art Warehouse. Without a stamp. I have not heard from Will since.

————————◆————————

On discussing this Act with some old anarcho-squatters from the '70s, they revealed that they would post breeze blocks to people they disliked, who, on receipt of the stampless package, had to pay for the delivery at the other end.

One day later I approach the counter staff at my local post office, who know me well, with a trial breeze block wrapped in brown paper.

'No, Mark,' they say as I offer them the package. 'If you want to send this to Mr Gove, you will need a stamp.'

Times have changed and it appears one can no longer send breeze blocks in the post. But you can …

ACT 4 … send roof tiles.

The tile slips snugly into a Jiffy bag, weighs quite a bit AND fits into a postbox.

So next time you go past a building site, arm up, then follow the rules:

| 1. INSERT ROOF TILE | 2. ADDRESS PACKAGE | 3. POST WITHOUT STAMP |

Be warned: it is a seriously addictive pastime. Just before Christmas my wife was walking down the street when she caught sight of me standing in the middle of a skip.

'What are you doing?' she asked incredulously.

I said, 'I'm looking for a reply to Virgin Media.'

ACT 5 In 2011 tax-avoiding bookseller Amazon acquired the DVD rental company LoveFilm *(now Amazon Prime Instant Video)* and with it the ire of many of the 10 million in the UK with hearing loss. While in the US Amazon's on-demand services provide subtitles, Amazon was refusing to do the same for its UK customers, or even provide information about which DVDs were already subtitled and which were not, making choosing a film a lottery if you are one of the 10 million. Why such a difference in policy, you ask? I have no idea except perhaps that Amazon is forced to subtitle in the US to comply with anti-discrimination legislation.

This prompted Stephanie McDermid to launch a petition on Change.org, calling on Amazon to behave with a semblance of dignity and provide accurate and comprehensive information about subtitled films. Despite 14,000 signatures Amazon would not even respond to letters from the chief executive of campaigning group Action on Hearing Loss.*

On the last day of the 100 Acts – **13 May 2014** – after locating Amazon's swanky new headquarters in Holborn, London, with the aid of some friends and a tallish lightweight aluminium ladder, we slapped a poster on the glass frontage of Amazon's HQ above the revolving entrance doors.

Photo: Chris Coltrane

AND … that evening Amazon announced a change in policy.

——————◆——————

---

* *The new name for the RNID.*

ACT 6 could have been so easily avoided if only Amazon had responded sooner. In the short period between putting the poster up and the company's response, I had sent Amazon Prime Instant Video's Vice President Tim Leslie a TV/DVD combo in the post, using their Freepost address.

The TV/DVD player had a note taped to it that read, 'Dear Amazon, without subtitles this isn't much use if you are deaf.' It weighed 11.41 kilograms, the largest Freepost committed in the 100 Acts.

Here are some of the other items sent in prepaid or unpaid packages:

LARGE HARDBACK   EARTH   CORN PLASTERS   BROKEN CLOCK

STONE (WITH A HOLE)   PLASTIC BAG   NEW PURITANS CD   OLD DOG BISCUIT

WEETABIX   SHOWER CURTAIN HOOPS   A FISH   HALF A BOX OF ALPEN

ACT 7 was inspired when a friend gave me a copy of a book called *One Day.** I loathed this book so much that it spawned a new form of heckling: book-heckling.

This is how you book-heckle:

1. Enter bookshop, browse.
2. Locate target book, pick book from the shelf.
3. Having prepared your heckle in advance *(on a smallish piece of paper, about the size of half a cigarette)* insert your heckle into the book, keeping the paper close to the spine to stop it falling out when opened.
4. Shut the book, place it back on the shelf.
5. Walk away.

On entering Waterstones – I don't take on local independent bookshops, just corporations – I head for Fiction and my target book *One Day*, open, insert heckle and exit.

Whoever bought that copy would have found a small piece of paper on page 36 with the words:

And then another on page 48:

BUT NOT SOON ENOUGH!

---

* One Day *a brief review: Richard Curtis thinks it's twee.*

Book-heckling is quite addictive, and soon others followed:

Book: *Fifty Shades of Grey* – Author: E. L. James
Location: Tesco – Page 46:

OTHER READERS PREFERRED
PROPER PORNOGRAPHY

Book: *The Enchantress of Florence* – Author: Salman Rushdie
Location: Waterstones – Page 146:

NO ONE WOULD KNOW IF YOU
STOPPED READING THIS

Book: *Inferno* – Author: Dan Brown
Location: WHSmith – Page 55:

THE PERSON WHO BOUGHT
YOU THIS AS A GIFT HATES YOU

Book: Any – Author: Ian Rankin
Location: WHSmith motorway service station – Page 67ish:

ADMIT IT, YOU THINK YOU MIGHT
HAVE READ THIS ONE BEFORE

Book: Any – Author: John Grisham
Location: Numerous – Page 1:

CONDITION OF SALE:
PLEASE LEAVE IN HOLIDAY COTTAGE

Book: The Bible – Author: Various
Location: bedside drawer, Premier Inn – Page iii:*

ALSO AVAILABLE IN ARABIC

A young woman sent me a photo of her book-heckle for Stephenie Meyer's *Twilight Saga: Breaking Dawn*:

If you are over 16, grow up
and buy Dracula

---

* *A friend goes one step further and he signs the title page: 'Thanks for your continued support, Jesus.'*

From book-heckling it was just a hop, a skip and a jump to ACT 8: book-stickering.

'Aha,' you may cry, 'bookshops already use stickers on their stock.' Indeed, and therein is the issue.

A book is a thing of potential wonder and beauty, a conduit of emotion, human knowledge and poetry, every book a potential gateway to situations and people we might otherwise know nothing of. Whoever decided to place a sticker on a book devalues its worth and reduces it to a commodity-like roof tile of chocolate knocked out on the cheap at the till.

A book might transform our lives, to quest for new horizons of truth and discovery, while a sticker will always reduce us to scratching chimps trying to peel them off.

Alongside motorists failing to indicate when they turn the corner and pensioners wearing training shoes for everyday wear, stickers on books are one of the signs of a decline in standards of community decency.

My first book-stickers were printed in the style and manner of a WHSmith sale. I idled into the shop, browsed through my target books and then gently applied my sticker. The remarkable thing is that there are so many stickers on books that any that you or I apply will meld into the plethora of inanities and adhesive that constitutes this pollution. No one will notice from a distance and it is only when you pick up the book that you will read:

The second sticker and ACT 9 was inspired by an ex-politician's autobiography:

Some people created their own stickers. One was on a Jamie Oliver recipe book: it read, '10p from this book sale goes to the Save Jamie Appeal'.

Another was placed on a Dan Brown novel. It read, 'CAUTION increasingly implausible storyline'.

However, the truly Zen art of book-stickering is not printing your own stickers or using mine, but using the bookshop's own stickers against it.

Simply peel off the bookshop's own stickers and place them on other books. I recommend you start off with the Bible and a sticker with the words 'Author signed copy'.

The final book-sticker **ACT 10** was created with only one book in mind – the debut novel from game-show contestant and sexual-abstinence campaigner Nadine Dorries MP, *The Four Streets*:

There are enough promotional adverts in the world, but not enough to dissuade you from buying a product. The QR code on this sticker links directly to a review of her book by Sarah Ditum in the *New Statesman* magazine. Try it.

Photos of deployed stickers as tweeted by various audience members.

ACTS 11-16

COPS & CAMERAS

As I drew up plans for starting 100 Acts, I knew I wanted to have one continuous Act. It needed to be something that would plunge me into the spirit of the project and potentially put me at conflict with authority on a regular basis. ACT 11 seemed to fulfil those requirements.

Here are the rules:

1. I must photograph a police officer every weekday for a year.
2. The photo must be taken in front of them from a distance of no more than five metres from the officer.
3. The police officer must know they are being photographed.
   NB: *The officer should look directly at me at some point during the process to confirm Rule 3 is complied with.*
4. I must be polite at all times.
5. I can't reveal the purpose of taking the photo to the officer.

14 May 2013 – Day 1: A little worried about this. There is a sometimes tricky art to handling the police: a mixture of confidence, legal knowledge and agility, but most of all knowing when to piss off. Deciding the capital's centre will be the most obvious place to find police officers to photograph, I head into Oxford Circus and spend a cop-free hour wandering. Sure enough there are police in cars, on bikes and in vans, but none cross my path on foot.

'A tourist area,' I almost say out loud and get the Tube to Victoria Station; there are bound to be police officers there.

I leave the Tube carriage, climb the escalator and at the top, as the rails are sliding into the metal grill, I look up and two officers are standing by the ticket machine. Panic. Camera bag is locked. Use phone. Open case.

Put in code. Bring camera app up. My hand has tremors but I approach the police, stand directly in front of the officers, two metres from them, and as I take the photo a thickset officer with a square jaw fixes me directly with his eyes. We lock glances, he stares at me and I at him, then he smiles, wide-eyed, and gives the thumbs up for the picture.

I am happy to share that unexpected delight and happier still to inform you that of all the photos I took for this Act, 27% featured what I came to refer to as 'smiley cops'.

On seeing one PC outside Burger King on Balham Hill carrying a milkshake and a carton, I said, 'Excuse me,' holding up the camera. The officer grinned and held the milkshake in the air, striking the pose of the Statue of Liberty.

Striding through Leeds station one morning, I spied a PC and hurriedly snapped his image. He stood stock still then bellowed, 'Mark Thomas! Bloody legend!' in a broad Yorkshire accent, then said, 'Come on, I've got to get one of us together.'

Which is how I ended up in a selfie with my arm around a police officer in rush hour.

Most officers, 55% in all, were brusque or indifferent, which is fine as they have a job to do and we don't need to be best friends.

However 18% of the police photographed were 'arsey'. Now you may ask, 'Mark, what is your definition of arsey in this context?'

It means attempting to stop me photographing them, either being physically or verbally intimidating, or misrepresenting the law as to suggest or directly state it is illegal to photograph them, essentially stopping someone going about their lawful business with no good cause or legal reason ... arsey.

There are many reasons for wanting to photograph a police officer every weekday for a year, not just because it is legal to do so – though some police may not have heard *(see overleaf)* – but because of the behaviour of the police Forward Intelligence Teams (FITs). These police surveillance teams monitor, photograph and video demonstrations and the protestors who attend them, and have a reputation for intimidation and harassment.

> **Andrew Carter** was arrested after taking a photo of a police officer who ignored a 'no entry' sign. He received an apology from the police.

> **Jules Mattsson** was awarded £4,000 in compensation from the Met Police and an apology for being arrested while trying to take pictures during an Armed Forces Day parade in London. This sum also includes compensation for having homophobic language used against him.

> **Gemma Atkinson** was arrested for filming her boyfriend being stopped and searched. Police settled the case in 2010.

Another reason for this Act is that I am monitored by the police and if they can do it to me, I can do it to them.

Quite reasonably, many of you may be raising your eyebrows and possibly thinking of phrases that involve the words 'paranoid', 'delusional' and 'nutter alert' – that is, of course, if you have not thought these things already. Stating the police monitor me is quite a bold claim to make, but it's made on the basis I have the evidence and am taking them to court.

———————◆———————

I am one of about 9,000 people in the UK given the official classification 'domestic extremist' by the police. This sounds a confusing conflation of words. We know I am extreme, but in what context? After all there is such a thing as extreme fishing, but to the best of my knowledge, Robson

Green has yet to publicly announce a desire to set up a caliphate by violent means while landing a marlin off the coast of Florida. The context for my extremism is 'domestic' – possibly a kitchen radical, perhaps I cook naked or use full-fat milk *and* butter. Fortunately MI5 have issued a definition:

> **Domestic extremism** mainly refers to individuals or groups that carry out criminal acts of direct action in pursuit of a campaign. They usually aim to prevent something from happening or to change legislation or domestic policy, but try to do so outside of the normal democratic process.

At this point I have a confession to make to you: contrary to the image people have of me, in actual fact I have no criminal record.

None.

Surprising to some, but true nonetheless. Perhaps as surprising is the fact that I have helped the police put someone in jail; I reported an illegal arms dealer to the police who was arrested, tried, convicted and served time. So I don't quite know why I am a 'domestic extremist'. What I do know is that once deemed a 'threat', the National Domestic Extremism and Disorder Intelligence Unit (NDEDIU) can put a person under surveillance and monitor and collect information on them for their files.

How do I know I am on this list? The first clue came in 2005 when my picture appeared on a police spotter card – a collection of FIT photos on a single laminated sheet issued to police to more easily identify 'domestic extremists' at demos. Not the greatest photo and frankly Equity should have sued them for not using my best side.

However the main evidence comes from **ACT 12**. I apply for the information the police hold on me under the Data Protection Act 1998 and, 70 days after making the application *(30 days past the legal deadline – just saying)*, I receive some of the contents of my file from the police.

There are 63 entries in all and they look like this:

> 07/12/2008
> NO SWEAT GATHERING
> People's Palace Queen Mary Westfield College London with Mark Thomas among speakers.
>
> ---

Speaking at conference on sweatshops. They are monitoring me for this? If they are watching me then Oxfam must be crawling with undercover cops.

> 28/01/1999
> Cricklewood Against Nuclear Trains (CANT)
> Comedian Mark Thomas (Ch5 Wednesday) will be recording a show on this topic on Sunday for showing on 03/02/1999.
>
> ---

Nice that my old TV shows are considered examples of domestic extremism.

> Stop the War coalition is holding a conference on 01/12/2007, at Westminster, Central Hall, London. Confirmed speakers at the conference: Mark Thomas, Comedian.
>
> ---

Speaking at a conference is domestic extremism?!?! A million people marched in central London to stop the war in Iraq.

24/02/2007
Stop the War march ... TRAFALGAR SQUARE
About 1408 hours we spotted Mark THOMAS who is a comedian ...
THOMAS was on a silver mountain bike with yellow forks an orange
bib with Protestor written on back and a white cycle helmet. He said
hello to us as he passed and seemed very happy.

Favourite! Love that they are monitoring my bike and dress code as well
as my emotional well-being. I read it out loud in a Pathé newsreel voice
as an experiment and, yes, this really is the Stasi meets Ealing comedy.

08/09/2008
Student Union at the Open University (OU), Milton Keynes -
12.30hrs on Tues 09/09/08 (against the better wishes of the OU
management) have invited Mark Thomas, a political comedian, to
speak in the Beryl Lecture Theatre. He is quite outspoken about
several issues including the arms trade.

The Open University management are reporting my book readings to
the police?!?!

09/03/2007
In the weekly LONDON edition of the 'TIME OUT MAGAZINE', there
is an article written by MARK THOMAS a political activist comedian,
advertising a MASS LONE DEMONSTRATION to be held on
WEDNESDAY 21/03/2007. His website also advertises this event.

Why is journalism on legal peaceful demonstration still on a file?

03/03/2009
CLASS WAR held a BASH A BILLIONAIRE event at the
DORCHESTER HOTEL PARK LANE ... The only identified protestor
was general rabble rouser and alleged comedian MARK THOMAS

Brilliant! 'Alleged Comedian' ★☆☆☆☆ *the Met Police*. Review from police arts correspondent. I am using that quote!

NB: Seems churlish to mention I have never attended a Class War demo. Would loved to have been on one but their demos always seem to clash with the Heal's sale.

01/05/2000
MD2K event, Parliament Square.
Mark Thomas (TV presenter and activist) stops to stand in the way
of the camera, has quantity of cress on rear of his cycle.

Cress. FUCKING CRESS!! The cops are monitoring garnish on my bike rack! Seriously? Taxpayers money is spent monitoring my fucking bicycle for CRESS!!!!!!

What do they think I am? ... the 'Picnic Wing' of al-Qaeda?

It goes on and on, and it's worth just reiterating I have no criminal record. I have taken legal action against the police and won for an unlawful stop and search. So, technically speaking, it is they who have a criminal record.

———————◆———————

Perplexed at my official classification as a threat to public order, the rule of law and indeed democracy itself, I threw myself at the mercy of my lawyer. He sits meticulously reading the documents the police sent to me, he lifts his head from the papers, places his glasses on the table, pauses appearing to collect his thoughts, then says, 'After reading the files, it is my honest legal opinion that the Metropolitan Police are fucked.'

We start planning ACT 13, and on **6 November 2014** my lawyer begins legal action against the Metropolitan Police Service.

Let me be clear, it is absolutely necessary to monitor potential terrorist and criminal activity. However, from my files it appears the police continue to monitor me, a person with no criminal record, collude with universities and private security forces to collect information, retain data about my occasional journalism and note my garnish of choice, not because I represent any real criminal threat, but because I have the audacity to be an occasional campaigner. I think it entirely reasonable to want them to stop and to remove me from the National Domestic Extremist Database, and in light of that to issue a judicial review on police policy and practice, and let the court decide. Either that or convert, train and kill the kuffar!

Joke!

I am one of a growing number of people taking legal action against police spying, including my five co-claimants in my case. All of us are members of the National Union of Journalists (NUJ) and all of us are classified as domestic extremists. Oh, and all of us cover stories of police and corporate malpractice … Oh yeah, and all of us have won cases against the police.

The NUJ legal action against the Met involves six NUJ journalists who individually applied for their files under the Data Protection Act:

Jules Mattsson, *The Times* journalist. In his file the police wrote:

> Officers need to be aware that although very well spoken, polite,
> curious and a little dramatic, Mr MATTSSON is always looking
> for a story.

Unlike proper journalists who get their stories the proper way by bribing police officers.

Adrian Arbib, professional photographer, has worked for the BBC, Reuters and occasionally the tabloids. He was stopped and questioned while photographing an apple orchard for a feature in the *Guardian* magazine on the decline of the English apple.

The incident is recorded thus:

> ARBIB above is a known environmental protestor ...
> Mr ARBIB appears to be a professional photographer

They then add the enigmatically pejorative phrase:

> with an interest in the environment and the like.

David Hoffman is vice chair of the British Photographic Council and has photographed some of the most iconic images from protests for 30 years. Somewhat ironically, the photograph the police have of him on their files was downloaded from the far-right website Redwatch, which is a racist site specialising in posting the names, photos and addresses of people the racists believe are enemies and traitors. So when looking for a photo of David for their files someone in the police thought, 'Oh, I know a website that will have him on.'

Jess Hurd's file includes this description:

> Jessica HURD - this is the female IC1 photographer with cropped [sic] hair and who always wears 'Joe 90' style thick black framed spectacles.

Jason N. Parkinson is a video journalist. His domestic extremist file notes that he was:

> Seen taking photographs of the students

… on a national student march. So the police have him on file for doing his job. His file also contains this entry:

> 18/08/2007
> CLIMATE CAMP
> Sightings/Stop Checks. Jason PARKINSON inside the camp.

… he was in Mexico at the time.

The legal challenge claims the police do not have the right to monitor NUJ members and journalists for doing their job under the European Convention on Human Rights, including Article 8 on privacy, Article 10 on freedom of expression, and Article 11 on freedom of assembly and association. The court action wants to see our files destroyed and the practice of spying on journalists ended.

———————◆———————

A Freedom of Information request in 2014 revealed that when the words 'domestic', 'extremist' and 'journalist' were entered into the police computers, over 2,000 entries were found. Which suggest more journalists being monitored by the police, and the only way to find out is for journalists to apply for their files. So **ACT 14**, an article for the NUJ website asking journalists to join our campaign, apply for their files and, if they are 'domestic extremists', to join our legal case.

In fact anyone can apply for data held about them by a public body or a corporation, or indeed an employer, using the Data Protection Act. If you want to do so, there is a template letter on page 179.

So that is where this story ends for the time being, except for one thing. In this tale of skulduggery, spying, power and arrogance there remains an unanswered mystery, a strand left flailing in the wind of deception. In this riddle of misdeeds wrapped in the bed sheets of mistrust there is an unsolved conundrum: what to do with the hundreds of photos I have taken of the police?

Well, it would seem churlish and spiteful to do something publicly with the photos of the smiley cops.

During the Edinburgh festival I photographed one cop who said, 'How's the show going, Mark?'

'Well, thank you.'

'I'm coming to see you next week. I look forward to finding out about the photo.' And he did too.

It seems unfair to use their images. Likewise the busy and indifferent cops – they were working and doing their jobs.

As for the arsey cops?

I brought out a calendar. The calendar is called, 'Arsey Cops'.* Producing it and selling it by the cartload was **ACT 15**.

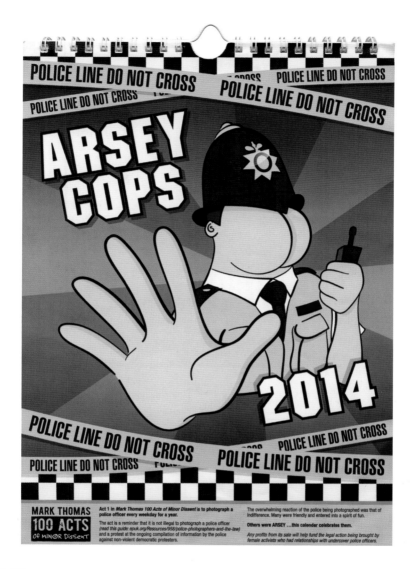

ACT 16 was giving all the profits from the sale of the calendars to another legal action brought by female campaigners duped into relationships with undercover police officers. I wish them good luck.

ACTS 17-20

SHELF-BARKERS & SHOPLIFTERS

barker*

/ˈbɑːkə/ *NOUN informal*
A tout at an auction, sideshow, etc.,
who calls out to passers-by to attract custom.

shelf-barker**

1. Shop propaganda designed to encourage
   shoppers to buy more. Often misleading.
2. Eye pollution.

I got friend and designer Greg Matthews to create our own shelf-barkers for **ACT 17**, mimicking the style, font and logo of the appropriate supermarkets. We printed them out and inserted them into the plastic holders.

The first supermarket was Tesco, and I started in the dairy section. At about eye height I inserted a barker that somewhat philosophically read:

Photo: Dan Mudford

* Oxford English Dictionary.
** *Dictionary of Mark Thomas.*

The next was inserted in the wines and spirits section:

Photo: Greg Matthews

Others included:

45

Tesco was not the only target. The Waitrose shelf-barker stayed by the Fairtrade bananas for three days:

Wishing to extend the joy of guerrilla shelf-barking, I invited people to submit haikus via Twitter, printed them up and placed them in Sainsbury's. I called ACT 18 'Talking Poetry to the Rack Man'.

This was by the root vegetables:

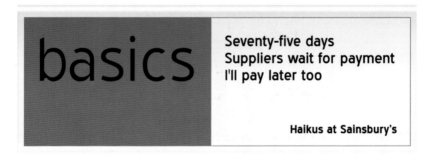

As a consequence of committing 100 Acts, people often credit me with something I haven't done. Five months after placing the shelf-barkers, other versions began to appear, including one in Tesco demanding increased wages for workers in the store, using their tag line, 'Every Little Helps'.

They looked absolutely legit until you read the slogan.

Whoever did that one *SALUT!* and thank you.

ACT 19 Any decent-minded person enters Harrods with only one intention and that is to be removed from the premises. One afternoon, I enter the grocery-cum-department store accompanied by two comics, Angela Barnes and Gráinne Maguire. We walk around the shop, past the stationary, the ink wells and literally diamond-encrusted fountain pens. All three of us carry clipboards and make notes as we wander. All three of us are wearing hi-vis vests. On the back of my vest is printed:

SHOPLIFTER INSTRUCTOR

We have made notes of the exits and timed how long it would get to them. On the back of Angela and Gráinne's vests are the words:

TRAINEE SHOPLIFTER

I should add that the staff are very pleasant and, whether out of training, devilment or sheer good manners, one chap approaches me and says, 'Is there anything in particular you are after, sir?'

'Jewellery,' I reply.

'This way, sir,' he says and gestures us towards the bling.

The security descend upon us in 10 minutes and 53 seconds.

ACT 20 Selfridges, same people, same hi-vis vests – we last 20 minutes before they kick us out. Twenty minutes! We wander up every floor, we queue in the coffee shop for buns displaying SHOPLIFTER on our backs, we block the escalator at one point, loudly discussing the 'ethics of shoplifting British to support local produce'; still no one attempts to ask what we are doing there.

At one point we approach the sunglasses concession.

'Tell me, are these a popular brand?' I ask the sales person, pointing at a pair of shades.

'With our Arab clientele, very popular, sir.'

'Tell me,' I pause, 'what brand would a British bloke buy … say in … a pub?'

At this point security arrives. 'What do you think you are doing?!' says the angry plain-clothes man showing his badge.

'Er … browsing …'

Photo: Rikki Blue

48

ACTS 21-29

THE CURZONISTAS

FAIR PAY

ACT 21 I'm halfway through my year of dissent when I get a phone call. 'Is that Mark Thomas?'

'Yes.'

'Do you do Acts of Dissent by request?'

'It's not a bespoke service, but go on.'

'We work at the Curzon cinema.'

'Good.'

Now I love the Curzon, a proper art-house cinema chain: foreign films, discussions, LGBT and human-rights film festivals, and lots and lots and lots of documentaries. Black and white. Philip Glass soundtracks, all state-of-the-nation and plight-of-the-working-class stuff. The Curzon Soho has a coffee-and-cake concession run by Konditor & Cook, a baker so brilliantly middle class they have cake 'consultations'.

'We're members of BECTU* and we're fighting for the London living wage and trade-union recognition but the management won't recognise us.'

'WHAT? The management of the lovely liberal trendy Curzon cinema won't recognise a union?? That's outrageous! How can I help?'

'Will you write us a message of support?'

'Yes! I'd be happy to.'

'Will you write it on a radiogram board?'

'YES! ... What is a radiogram board?'

'It's the board that you hang the letters on outside the cinema.'

8.20 a.m. one lovely bright morning, my friend and collaborator Tracey Moberly and I arrive outside the Curzon Soho cinema, wearing a couple of hi-vis vests and carrying a tall lightweight aluminium ladder. We stand looking at the radiogram board. It reads:

ONE PM CENTRAL STANDARD TIME   Q & A SIR TREVOR MCDONALD MON 11 NOV 6.20
THE GREAT BEAUTY   GLORIA   BLUE JASMINE   SHORT TERM   12   THE SELFISH GIANT

---

* Broadcasting, Entertainment, Cinematograph and Theatre Union.

As we stare at the letters I say, 'We should have worked this out before we came.'

'Have you got a pencil and paper?' Tracey asks in her broad Welsh Valleys' lilt.

So we stand in the street in hi-vis vests, holding a large ladder, playing a rather awkward round of 'Countdown Conundrum'.

'What have you got?'

'Turtle nob jis.'

'That's not going to help.'

Sometime later we come up with:

Photo: Rikki Blue

The message was up for four hours before the management noticed, and I suspect that was only due to media calls after the photos began whizzing round social media.

Bizarrely, this was done in Shaftesbury Avenue, in the centre of London during rush hour, and no one questioned what we were doing.

My theory is, you can get away with most things if you are wearing a hi-vis vest. This is the great irony of hi-vis; once you have put it on you become invisible. Just another one of the countless outsourced zero-hero plebeians who are passed and ignored every day. Were burglars to eschew the traditional black apparel/balaclava combo and instead slip on a hi-vis jacket they would have a field day. We'd merely think, 'Who's that rummaging in the bedroom? … Must be the council … The jewellery inspector by the look of it.'

My 'hi-invisibility' theory is put to the test when performing ACT 22. Tracey and I take to the radiogram board again, this time at the Curzon Mayfair cinema. We had prepared our message in advance so spent a mere 10 minutes changing the letters, all the while under the watchful eye of the armed diplomatic police officers outside the Saudi Arabian Embassy opposite.

Hi-vis works its magic again! Though it was probably a good job those officers had not been on duty for the women's car race.

Our choice of letters was rather limited this time but we managed to write:

Photo: Rikki Blue

Our friends the *Curzonistas* were happy with our messages and with our methods of working. I could do things that would get *them* the sack, and the BECTU officials negotiating with Curzon could claim I was not officially representing BECTU. Everyone was happy except for the management, which is the way it should be. It was time to take the campaign to the audience. In the cinema. In the dark.

———————◆———————

ACT 23 A demonstration in a cinema is problematic. How do people see the demonstration? How do you protest without annoying the audience and without compromising the cinema workers on duty? And we haven't even begun to address the issue of who is going to pay for everyone's ticket to get in. The answer was the Day-Glo demos.

This is how they're done: you go into the Curzon cinema, you buy a ticket for the Curzon cinema, you sit down and when the lights lower you rush to the front of the screen *(preferably with friends)*, you lift up fluorescent banners and shine torches on them …

Photo: Rikki Blue

… and you hand out leaflets to the audience explaining we will only disturb the adverts and not the film AND explaining the cause of union recognition. That is how you Day-Glo demo.

When we leave the audience are so lovely, liberal and lefty they give us a round of applause. Several members of the audience write to Curzon management complaining … about the management. Hurrah!

> I was witness tonight to the Mark Thomas protest during the trailers before the 18.55 showing of Blue Jasmine at the Curzon Soho. The points raised were done so in a respectful manner and also completely correct. I, as a regular cinemagoer at Curzon, believe that your staff should be entitled to have BECTU negotiate on their behalf [and] have a decent wage.

And then my favourite bit … **ACT 24** we storm up to the box office and – in our best outraged *Daily Mail* reader voice – demand a refund because there has been a disturbance which has completed ruined our evening.

Photo: Chris Coltrane

I wasn't the only Curzon cinemagoer who was shocked by the low wages and lack of union recognition. Regular Fred Paxton set up a petition on Change.org on behalf of the *Curzonistas*, which got a lot of signatories and media attention, with Mike Leigh, Ken Loach and Will Self all lending their voice and their support.

Curzon were clearly feeling under pressure but, bizarrely, the Curzon management chose to write to me asking if they could explain their position, forgetting that my job is not to talk to them but to annoy them into speaking seriously with the union. Instead of replying I committed the second Day-Glo demo and we released a short film of the cinema workers explaining their cause, **ACT 25**. Naturally the workers had their identities concealed for fear of sacking, and naturally the home-made masks were film characters associated with unions and fair pay.

 www.vimeo.com/77865762

So, with the aid of a smartphone and set of headphones, demonstrators could quietly sit next to Curzon cinemagoers and show them the film before the main feature.

Photo: Michele Fenwick

ACT 26 After performing a show in Sheffield, I took the audience to the potential site for a new Curzon cinema there, a disused bank, and held an impromptu demonstration replete with banners. There is little point holding a demo at 11 at night, in a side street in Sheffield, unless there is documented evidence, so we photographed the demo and emailed Curzon's CEO, Philip Knatchbull, which in turn kicked off **ACT 27**.

I tour all over the country and at every show project the CEO's work email onto a screen, asking the audience to send him a polite and non-sweary message from their smartphones. Hundreds do. I know because each night the audience hold up their phones on completion of the task; a sea of blue glows from the auditorium indicating another batch of emails sitting in Phil Knatchbull's inbox. I also know because I put in a DPA request to Curzon – ACT 28 – and they send me back a heap of emails that reveal both the company's cool and collected response:

On 22 Oct 2013, Philip Knatchbull <█████████████> wrote:

█████████████████████████ AND Mark Thomas stood up and spoke against us at a Soho screening is now making a film. Oh Shit.

On 29 Nov 2013, ██████████████ wrote:

Thomas has evidently struck again in the early hours of the morning … Another hit of bad publicity and extra work for us to do. Is there any way we can press for criminal damage charges from this?'

And an email from an audience member who was far from polite and non-sweary:

From: David <██████████████>
Date: Sun, Dec 1, 2013 at 9:30PM
SUBJECT: CUNT
To: Philip Knatchbull <███████████████>

Mark Thomas says you might be a twat
I'm not sure either way

Naturally the CEO of Curzon cinemas objected to such abuse.

Curzon's response to my DPA request was processed in a slipshod and haphazard fashion, sending badly redacted emails that I could easily read if I held them up to the light, emails with third-party information that *should* have been redacted and notes made by management after interviewing members of staff about the radiogram board stunt. It was a bizarre collection, not least because it included a touching email from the CEO to his wife asking for her view on whether he was a cunt or a twat.

They didn't include her reply.

But they did include this:

On 2 Dec 2013, ███████████████ *wrote:*

I assume we've still heard nothing from Mark Thomas? I'd offer to help in making contact but I'm concerned that, if he saw there was a PR agency involved, it would only serve to inflame the situation.

… How right they were. I put in a DPA request to the PR agency who in turn had to pass on another bundle of data: ACT 29.

But we didn't just annoy Curzon with the petition and demos and emails. On **13 January 2014**, BECTU and Curzon issued a joint statement announcing a voluntary trade union recognition agreement and on **29 October 2014** Curzon became the first London cinema chain to pay their staff the London living wage.

———————◆———————

ACTS 30-34

RATS & PALACES

LIVING WAGE FOR CLEANERS

Some Acts of Dissent happened because I got cross with the news. They were not planned or part of a campaign, they were just instinctive reactions when I happened to be near a microphone, an audience and a projector.

Take the case of the MP Maria Miller: how could a woman who was done for fraud still be in her job? The independent Parliamentary Commissioner for Standards had recommended she repay £45,000. Please note the 'in' in 'independent' is pronounced silently here, as that sum was reduced to a mere £5,800 by the Commons Standards Committee. So MPs reduced the fine of a fellow MP to an eighth of the original figure.

Not only was she still in her job, not only did she have the fine slashed, but Miller's public apology in the House of Commons lasted 32 seconds. Thirty-two fucking seconds. Her morning shit took longer than her public apology for fraud.

Well fuck that, I thought. Backstage at the Playhouse theatre in Derry, I typed my own response into my computer and plugged it into the theatre projector system.

The second half of the show starts with ACT 30. Behind me is projected the words:

You're Bent. Go.

I ask the audience to photograph it and gave them her email address. By the following Wednesday she'd resigned.

I take no credit for her *volte-face*, but arriving to work to find 200 angry emails from Derry can't have hurt.

------------◆------------

ACT 31 follows the basic principles of ACT 30, namely losing my temper in the proximity of a projector. A friend sent me the advert below just before going onstage in Sale.

I promptly copied it into the computer and projected it to the crowd:

The South Leeds Academy
Unqualified Teacher of Maths x 2

Full Time / Term Time Only
Salary: UQT Points 1 - 6
Temporary until July 2014

We are seeking to appoint an enthusiastic, reliable, and self-motivated Unqualified Teacher of Maths to join The South Leeds Academy, starting as soon as possible.

The ideal candidates will possess a minimum of 4 GCSEs (Grades A* - C) including English and Mathematics or equivalent. Experience of working in a similar role would be desirable.

We look forward to you joining our dedicated and supportive team.

South Leeds Academy wanted *unqualified* teachers.

I assume because anyone who is anyone knows that the best sort of teachers are the unqualified ones; doncha know darling, all the best private schools are having them these days ... actually that might be true.

Qualifications? Health and safety gone mad!! What this world needs is common sense not qualifications. And, by God, South Leeds Academy will make sure your children get don't get them.

Put on your best Clarkson voice and bellow, 'Qualifications. I didn't get where I am with qualifications. Enthusiastic gentleman amateurs, that's what we need. Look how many air-traffic accidents happen with the professionals? It's time to give the amateurs and hobbyists a go! And don't get me started on surgeons.'

I asked the entire audience to apply for the job. And I have the feeling that most of them did, with the exception of one chap who spoke to me afterwards. He was a qualified teacher of maths and therefore ineligible.

The advert was withdrawn the following day.

Christmas came quickly in the cycle of the 100 Acts year – too quickly. I was seven months in and only approaching **ACT 32**, but even with the worry of having to pay the forfeit of £1,000 to UKIP I still found time to celebrate the season.

ACT 32 is a Christmas card. On the front is an adaptation of the John Lewis Christmas advert featuring the Hare and the Bear.

Hundreds of these cards were printed and teams of people placed them in the card racks in John Lewis stores.

The fact that the card was free probably pissed them off as well, going, as it does, against the spirit of Christmas.

If **John Lewis** can afford
to spend **£7 million**
on an **advert**

They can **afford to pay**
their **Cleaners**
a **Living Wage**

"I feel like a rat in a palace"

John Lewis cleaner

This card is a free gift in support of the cleaners who work
in John Lewis and are campaigning for a living wage as
enjoyed by many others in the John Lewis Partnership.

You can support them by signing this card and sending it to:

Sir Charlie Mayfield, Chairman
John Lewis Partnership
Carlisle Place, London SW1P 1BX

…or you can keep it to show your friends and
help raise awareness about the campaign.

Thank you and Merry Christmas!

There is a lot of like and hate in my relationship with John Lewis. I like buying clothes there but hate myself for it. For men of my age, shopping at John Lewis is a sartorial milestone, the point between Ben Sherman and the grave; the place where we slip into something more casual before slipping off altogether. It marks the point in our lives when we decide to let ourselves go.

I like sitting in their café area unmolested for the day, a middle-class hobo, a sort of Down and Out in Linens and Paris. On the other hand, I hate my fellow customers looking upon me as if I am collecting names for a Khmer Rouge re-education camp. I like the idea that the stores are a 'partnership', a progressive workplace where staff share in the profits, but hate that this is an illusion; that the cleaners have been outsourced, are not partners and do not even get the living wage, let alone a share in a bonus scheme.

ACT 33 Campaigners from the London Living Wage, some friends and I walk into Peter Jones in Sloane Square, Chelsea – this is the uber-posh John Lewis store; here they look down upon other John Lewis stores in much the same way as John Lewis customers look upon Lidl. We head up to the children's clothes and toys department. In the midst of which stands a cardboard cut-out woodland scene, complete with the Hare and the Bear from the adverts, and all their woodland friends smiling benignly to the customers and kids. Some with their arms in the air in joyous celebration of Christmas joy … empty arms that could hold something in them … say a banner … or placard.

Photo: Rikki Blue

Among the banners we place the rat cleaners: small cardboard rodents amid their woodland-dwelling betters.

A man in an impeccably pressed suit approaches me.

'Ah, Mr Thomas! I am a fan of your work.'

'Thank you.'

'I am the department manager, could you tell me what is going on?'

'It is a very polite protest about paying the cleaners the living wage.'

'Well I am going to have to remove your banners I am afraid.'

'They're only Blu-Tacked on so they should come off easily.'

The manager bends to remove the offending slogans but does not pick up the cleaner rats. 'As I say, I am a fan,' he continues as he picks at the Blu-Tack, 'but I do have to remove these.'

I point at the rats, 'You've missed some …'

'Oh thank you, I missed the … er …'

'Cleaners.'

'Yes, I missed the cleaners.'

'It might be appropriate to say, they are easy to miss.'

He looks at me from under his brow and smiles.

'Touché, Mr Thomas, touché.'

As we go to print, the John Lewis Partnership shows no sign of succumbing to the various campaigns, those run by the cleaners and civic society, so I commend the next Act of Dissent to you all.

Anyone who has been into Waitrose, the catering wing of John Lewis, will know of the green tokens or, as Waitrose describe it, their Community Matters scheme.

At the end of your shop, you receive a token to place in a box of the good cause you'd most like to support. The more tokens a cause gets, the bigger the donation they receive. Each month every Waitrose branch donates £1,000 *(£500 in convenience shops)* between three local good causes.

I'm ill inclined to applaud their charitable efforts when they seem so adamant on ensuring their cleaners are paid less than the living wage. Charity can never replace fairness. So for **ACT 34** I got 10,000 of these made and gave them out at shows. Some people may not want to go on a picket line or a demonstration, but anyone can put a token in a bin as a gesture of solidarity. If you want to join in, visit my website. I've just ordered another 10,000.

Photo: Greg Matthews

ACTS 35-41

BAN ME!!

As previously mentioned, at the end of my street is a branch of Tesco – most of the community were against it and opposed planning permission. The site of Tesco used to be a hospital and could so easily have been council houses *(you remember them)* or, shock horror, a hospital. Our community campaigned for eight years, organising petitions, delegations, lobbying councillors, investigating legal actions. We held meetings, socials and fundraisers. And finally lost when the then-CEO of Tesco's lobbied the government, who in turn put the pressure on the council.

And so the closed hospital was razed and a new Tesco erected, much to the disappointment of most of the residents.

When the new Tesco opened, what was the first thing they did? Put up a community noticeboard.

Cheeky bastards!

Since Tesco arrived, the grumpy old Italian guy who ran a deli has shut down. The off-licence shut down. And Tesco want to be part of our community? No one really wanted them, local businesses have suffered, their fucking apples come from Argentina. Exactly how community-minded are they?

Unfortunately they are cheap and they are up the road. Over the years I have gone from zero visits to probably once a week. This does not make me happy and so I started a series of Acts.

I walk into Tesco near Goodge Street in central London, and ask to speak to the manager – a nice chap and entirely smiley. I say to him, 'I wonder whether you might ban me?'

'What?' he says confused.

'Would you please ban me from Tesco?'

'What do you want to be banned for?'

'I am trying to explore a paradox: on one hand, multi-million corporate convenience shops are destroying the ecology of the high street and local businesses, affecting SMEs and disrupting the velocity of money in a local economy, AND, on the other hand, they are unfortunately extremely convenient and thus compromising to my politics of community. So I would like to be banned please.'

'Look,' he says becoming somewhat weary, 'if you don't like Tesco don't shop here.'

'Ah,' I reply, 'that is a boycott and it leaves me doing all the work. I want you to shoulder some of the effort. I want you to ban me.'

The Tesco manager smiles kindly, runs his hand through his hair, takes a deep breath and says, 'I can't ban you but this is what I can do. Next time you come in here, ask for me, and I will physically push you out of the shop. Does that work for you?'

Photo: Vanessa Furey

'So, if I have this correctly, you will not ban me?'

'No I will not.'

'But you will physically assault me?'

'Yes.'

After asking politely to be banned and failing, I take to the streets, protesting outside the store: ACT 35.

ACT 36 saw my second attempt – another day, another Tesco. Deferential and polite, I ask the deputy manager, Martin, 'I wonder if you might ban me, please?'

'I'm not going to ban you,' says Martin, somewhat confounded by the request.

'Can I ask why not?'

'Well, you haven't done anything wrong. To get banned,' he explains, 'you have to do something wrong, like assault the staff or swear or shoplift.'

'I'm not going to do those things. They are anti-social and I don't want to get into trouble; I just want to get banned.'

'Well I can't ban you unless you have done something wrong,' he insists.

'Aha!' I start. 'Will you come with me for a moment.'

Martin dutifully and patiently accompanies me to the fruit and veg aisle where I show him this:

Photo: Mark Thomas

Martin's instant response is to laugh.

'Well,' I say when he starts to calm down, 'does this get me banned?'

'No,' he giggles.

'Why not?'

'Because it's funny.'

'That is not fair—'

'Oh, hang on,' he interrupts, 'you have graffitied our oranges.'

'They're not yours. I paid for them, wrote on them, brought them in here and have a receipt. I told you, I don't want to get into trouble.'

'Well I definitely can't ban you.'

He didn't respond to the shelf-barkers either.

Once more I take to the street, though this time with a petition asking people to sign it to get me banned. Over the coming weeks I get 1,000 signatures and send it to Tesco's head office; they do not reply to **ACT 37** and I still await their official response.

Undeterred by the corporation's rebuffs, I respond with **ACT 38**: it is simple and ineffective. I stood there for 20 minutes; eventually a security guard came over and asked if I was OK.

It was time to take consumer activism to a new level: **ACT 39**. I went shopping with a bamboo cane. This is how you do it: enter the store with a bamboo cane and start your shop with an item of fruit with a thick skin, like a grapefruit or large orange. Place the fruit onto the bottom of your bamboo, making sure it is firmly attached – this will form your

71

Photo: Chris Coltrane

Photo: Chris Coltrane

stopper. Move on to items with holes in them, such as doughnuts and pretzels, leaving items with cardboard packaging and loaves of bread to be skewered in the middle, and then top off the cane with a soft item like cheese.

At the till the assistant smiled and asked me, 'Why are you shopping with a stick.'

'I hate plastic bags.'

'Oh I know, I hate them too,' she replied.

Still no ban.

So far polite requests, petitions and demos had failed. At this point I turned to the late Hunter S. Thompson for inspiration and found it in a quote from The Gonzo Papers, Book 1: *The Great Shark Hunt: Strange Tales from a Strange Time* (1979), 'When the going gets weird the weird turn pro.' I am not sure Mr Thompson would have approved of my efforts as the Act involved no drugs or firearms, however ACT 40 was inspired by his quote.

Photo: Chris Coltrane

There are not many men in their fifties who can pull off wearing a Dalmatian onesie. There are fewer still that can wear one with dignity while pulling a skateboard on a piece of string behind them with a whole salmon taped to the board while in store browsing.

I know this because I am not one of them. Twenty-five minutes I wandered the aisles in Tesco, before the manager approached me cautiously and asked, 'Can I help you with anything, sir?'

'Well, if it is not too much trouble, can you ban me?'

'Oh it's you,' he mutters and disappears. Leaving me wandering near the refrigerators.

The only person to give me any flak was a woman who said to me, 'That's not a very nice way to treat that creature.'

'You should see what they do to his mates, the tuna, in aisle 3,' I replied.

Still no ban … drastic action was called for.

ACT 41: THE BAN PLAN

Equipment needed:
- Large pair of scissors
- Large bulldog clip
- Large wheelie suitcase
- Tupperware boxes to fit into suitcase
- Plastic rubbish bags
- Tin opener

Method:
1. Enter Tesco and select item to purchase
2. Open packaging and transfer contents into Tupperware box
3. Place Tupperware box in suitcase
4. Cut the barcode from the packaging and place it in the bulldog clip; put bulldog clip and barcode in pocket
5. Put packaging into plastic rubbish bag and trail it behind the wheelie suitcase
6. Repeat until stopped

The methodology was executed with the following items:
- Blueberries
- Bananas
- Box of Alpen
- Pack of coffee beans
- Mr Kipling French Fancies *(paper wrapping removed on all six fancies and placed in rubbish bag)*
- Babybels *(red waxy casing removed)*
- Cup a Soup *(all four sachets emptied into Tupperware)*
- Cat food *(all twelve sachets emptied into the Tupperware)*

Observations:

While squeezing the last sachet of cat food into the Tupperware box Mark Thomas was approached by the Tesco manager.

TM: Excuse me sit what are you doing?

MT: Shopping.

TM: Have you paid for those items?

MT: No, but I will do. I have saved all the barcodes.

TM: I am afraid you can't do that. You have to pay and leave please, sir. You will have to stop this now please.

MT: There's some beans and tinned soup I want.

TM *(to colleague)*: Security please.

MT: Are you kicking me out?

TM: Once you have paid for the items.

MT: Are you banning me?

TM: Yes.

MT: You are banning me?

TM: Yes.

MT goes to till with bulldog clip of barcodes, pays for items, leaves rubbish bag with helpful member of staff.

Results:

Banned from Tesco.

VICTORY!

Though as I stood there clutching a Tupperware box full of cat food, I thought, 'Who really is the winner here?'

Photos by: Vanessa Furey, Chris Coltrane, Sam Riddle.

ACTS 42-48

SEDITIOUS STROLLING & SUSPICIOUS SALMON

Despite my protestations of having no criminal record *(see* **ACTS 11–16***)* I did actually break the law in Tesco and it all started with the royal family.

I am neither a fan of the British monarchy nor the obsequious fawning that accompanies it. As far as I can make out, royal state occasions are essentially ring-kissing orgies of grovelling made decorous by the presence of gowns, wigs and Latin. It is the kind of arse-to-face contact not seen outside *The Human Centipede*, but bung a bit of ermine over it and chuck in a few prayers and apparently it's the kind of tradition that is the envy of the world.

Many actually believe the utter nonsense spouted to justify the Windsors' position: that the royals are decreed royal, by God. Think this through friends; this would mean Prince Philip was subject to divine intervention and chosen by God. That is the official line. God picked him. In any sane world Philip wouldn't be a prince, he would be a minicab driver and a UKIP candidate expelled for bringing the party into disrepute.

Frankly, we should have done with them all.

So you can imagine my delight when I found out that my views are illegal. Yes, these views are illegal.

The Treason Felony Act 1848 is still on the statute books and has never been repealed. As such it remains law, and Section 3 of the Treason Felony Act 1848 states:

IF ANY PERSON WHATSOEVER SHALL, within the UNITED KINGDOM or without, compass, imagine, invent, devise, or intend to deprive or depose our MOST GRACIOUS LADY THE QUEEN, from the style, honour, or royal name of the imperial crown of the UNITED KINGDOM . . . shall express, utter, or declare, by publishing any printing or writing . . . or by any overt act or deed, every person so offending shall be guilty of FELONY, and being convicted thereof shall be liable . . . to be transported beyond the seas for the term of his or her natural life.

In other words, it is illegal to declare and print anti-monarchist sentiment, indeed it is illegal even to imagine it. Just picturing them in your mind working for a living is technically illegal. Note it is also illegal to 'move or stir any foreigner' to do likewise. Not just illegal but treasonable too. I don't know how this knowledge affects you, but right now I have an erection.

Having composed myself and safe with this knowledge, I write to the Royal Parks in London, as I am legally obliged to do so, seeking their permission for a march from Admiralty Arch to Buckingham Palace, envisioning an end of the British monarchy.

I describe the event for them:

> Walking along the pavement, approximately 18 people will silently imagine an end to the British monarchy. The procession will be silent – there will be no banners, slogans or chanting. Essentially we are a small group of people quietly walking down the pavement. Imagining the end of the British monarchy.

On **13 March 2014** the manager of the Royal Parks replied:

> I regret I am unable to grant permission for your procession.

I reflect on the notion that some Acts of Dissent say more about the status quo than the dissenter as I walk down the Mall. Accompanied by a small group of friends we all quietly think of ending the British monarchy, thereby committing a felony punishable by deportation. More than that, we meet some German tourists at Buckingham Palace and encourage them to overthrow the monarchy as well, thus stirring a foreigner to end the Windsors' rule. Add to that a breach of the Park's by-law and we have three offences, but I count it as one – ACT 42.

I am well aware that none of this took place in Tesco and have thus far shed little light onto my claim as to breaking the law in the supermarket.

However, **ACT 42** was to prove to be just the starting point as I delved into the realm of unrepealed old laws still on the statute books. With the help of Tracey *(the artist from the Valleys)*, my old tour manager PD *(a large gentleman from the East End of the city)* and a kindly array of friends, I plan to commit as many offences from one old law as possible in the course of a day.

The law in question is the Metropolitan Police Act 1839, Section 54, Prohibition of nuisances by persons in the thoroughfares, Article 8, which states that it is an offence to:

> . . . roll or carry any cask, tub, hoop, or wheel, or any ladder, plank, pole, showboard, or placard, upon any footway, EXCEPT for the purpose of loading or unloading any cart or carriage . . .

The morning starts with **ACT 43**, carrying a plank on a footway. Yes, a plank. Read the list above again – it is illegal to carry a plank. Man I am so bad you can practically hear the old-school beats blasting from my pimped SUV. The plank in question is a scaffold board but it seems a tad tame to just walk with it through the streets, so Tracey paints the words 'THIS IS A HECKLE' in large white letters on it and I carry the board across London, straight to the Tate Britain and walk straight in *(hi-vis blazing)*, place it in the gallery and leave. The plank was on display for about 25 minutes. People came and looked at it, viewed it from different angles, stroked their chins, and *Time Out* gave it four stars.

Photo: Tracey Moberly

For my next Act in this law-breaking cavalcade of riotous rebellion, I decide to carry a pole. The most difficult part of ACT 44 is finding a decent pole; a 16-foot barge pole is hard to come by in London but I manage. With the pole hastily fastened to the roof of my old tour manager's van, Tracey and I cross town to the head office of Wonga.com.

We place the pole by the entrance of the building, then fix a poster to Wonga's door.

As an aside, Article 10 of the Metropolitan Police Act prohibits, 'Every person who, without the consent of the owner or occupier, shall affix any posting bill or other paper against or upon any building, wall, fence.'

This is
wonga HQ

If you *must* touch them, please use the long pole provided

Photo: Tracey Moberly

So technically that's two offences.

The day is spent pelting from one location to another, with Tracey making props as we go along, friends helping find materials we need and PD narrowly avoiding a driving ban. Lunchtime sees Tracey and I wheeling a set of tyres along the street (*another breach of the law and* ACT 45) towards … the Saudi Arabian Embassy.

The police look concerned when Tracey arrives, bent double, pushing a tyre along the pavement like a toy.

'We're just doing some photos,' I say to the officers, passing Tracey my tyre and unhooking the camera from around my neck. Tracey takes up position in front of the embassy gates, standing by the crossed swords in iron in her overalls. She hefts one tyre in the air, leaving the other hanging by her side, replicating Herb Ritts' iconic *(and somewhat homoerotic)* image 'Fred with Tires'.

The police officers look anxious. 'She's not going to expose herself is she?' says one.

'What?' I splutter.

'Seriously, she can't get her kit off.'

'She's not going to.' I shake my head and continue to photograph, whereupon another officer asks, 'She's not going to take her top off?'

Tracey's broad Welsh vowels cut their enquiries down. 'Don't be soft,' she barks.

Photo: Tracey Moberly Archive

I can only assume that the diplomatic protection squad have had a tip-off about a topless attack involving a boob-bearing, bomb-waving zealot. Though I have not heard of this tactic being previously deployed by al-Qaeda, who I assume do not have an armed 'Stunna' wing.

We leave the embassy slightly confused but having broken the law, completed the Act, and safe in the knowledge that if a woman driving upsets the diplomats they are probably foaming at the mouth at the thought of a woman changing a tyre.

———————◆———————

PD is parked around the corner and we dump the tyres and head to Piccadilly, to play an annoying game in a public thoroughfare – another illegal activity – and thus commit ACT 46. A gaggle of chums assemble by Piccadilly Tube station entrance. We assemble a makeshift table and chairs and start to play a game of Risk as passers-by look on, mostly indifferent, though some tut and one asks to join in.

Photo: Sam Riddle

I am not sure if our actions were annoying, but Risk is definitely an annoying game and it finishes after half an hour when I abandon the rules, declare myself benign dictator and smash the other players' pieces.

Kindly, some friends gather up the remains of the game, while Tracey and I grab a ladder, a placard and a whole salmon and set off for Tesco.

Yup, that's me and the salmon in **ACT 40**.

For the sake of order let's quickly deal with the fact that walking with a ladder and the placard *(later used outside Tesco, standing on top of the ladder, holding the banner in my onesie)* is illegal and becomes **ACT 47**.

And to return to the salmon. There is such a thing as the Salmon Act 1986 – a fairly recent law – and Article 34 of said law makes it is illegal to handle a salmon in suspicious circumstances. So how could I handle a salmon in suspicious circumstances?

I could buy two seats at the opera and sit with the salmon next to me during a performance of *Rigoletto*, telling audience members that, 'It's one of his favourites,' and not to worry if he cries.

I could speed down a motorway and when I get pulled over by the police swap seats with the salmon.

I could make a salmon thong and walk naked but for the fish covering my privacy, and try to get into the public gallery in the House of Commons.

I could have done any of these things and not only break the law but possibly be sectioned.

In the end it was breaking the law with a salmon on a skateboard, in a onesie, in Tesco, that won out for **ACT 48**.

In one day I have wilfully broken the law eight times and committed treason, an offence punishable with deportation – nothing will get me off the domestic extremist list now. Who knows, perhaps as I write these very words MI5 are monitoring the salmon run, watching these spawning returnees, ever vigilant for salmon heading home via Syria.

ACTS 49-56

MIND THE FARAGE

(PRONOUNCED: FARRIDGE)

ACT 49 On occasion, one or two of the 100 Acts made the news and I found myself back in the local press.

Local news site *Kent Online* broke its scoop in this fashion:

> Mystery shrouds changes made to controversial UKIP posters in Folkestone, after stickers offering alternative slogans were plastered over the originals.

I did it. No mystery.

> A disgruntled resident has decided to rewrite the messages on them.

It was ME! Not a resident!

> One of the alterations reads: "Have you tried hating foreigners? ... We think you'll like it".

> Another replies to UKIP's suggestion EU laws are hitting British workers with "unlimited cheap labour" by saying instead that UKIP is: "keeping low paid jobs for British workers".

———————◆———————

Who really runs this country?

75% of our laws are now made in Brussels.*

HAVE YOU TRIED HATING FOREIGNERS? ...WE THINK YOU'LL LIKE IT

Photo: A. MacLaren

EU policy at work.

British workers are hit hard by unlimited cheap labour.

KEEPING LOW PAID JOBS FOR BRITISH WORKERS

Photo: A. MacLaren
JCDecaux

Ever on the trail of truth and justice *Kent Online* reports four days later that Kent Police are investigating the matter.

> UKIP county councillor for Folkestone, Frank McKenna, said he had contacted the police about the vandalism to the posters. They had advised him the nature of some of the comments daubed on the billboards constituted a hate crime and would investigate on that basis.

Hah! A hate crime no less. Wow! The police have totally got the hang of this hate-crime business. Though on reflection, semantically they are right.

Anyway the mystery is solved. I did it. I now ask for another two Acts to be taken into consideration: **ACT 50** and **ACT 51**.

In the back of the taxi, heading from Harrogate railway station to the DIY store, I ask the driver if there is much support for UKIP in the area.

'Quite a bit I'd say,' he opines in a soft Yorkshire lilt.

'What about UKIP billboards. Have you seen many of them about?'

'Oh no, not billboards, no.'

Shocked at the distaste he has expressed, I ask, 'Why?'

'Not round here, that'd be gauche.'

Gauche, no less. I want to reply, 'You've mistaken me for Alan Bennett.' Instead I say, 'People must put up posters in the windows though?'

'Some. There are UKIP placards people put on their lawns or in plant pots.'

'That's very tasteful.'

'It is.'

'Perhaps UKIP should do paper doilies and put them out in tea rooms.'

'Very good idea.'

To be honest we don't chat a huge amount after that, especially after he informs me, 'People think Harrogate is a Conservative area but it's not, you know. Oh no.'

Then in a voice approaching a male Patricia Routledge he adds, 'We've got a BNP councillor.'

That night Tracey the Artist and I go looking for UKIP posters to adjust. True to the taxi driver's word, there are none in Harrogate that we can find; it does appear that the presence of a UKIP billboard would indeed be a veritable gaucherie.

So we head to Leeds to hunt down posters, dressed in all-in-one zip-up hooded Ebola suits and hi-vis vests, armed with the aluminium lightweight ladder and some spray cans. Wandering around the ring road at 2 a.m. we find our first poster. Next to a picture of a finger pointing at the reader it says:

26 million people in Europe are looking for work. And whose jobs are they after?

'Right,' I say to Tracey, 'we have to argue that this is preposterous. Unemployed people go where the work is, 26 million people aren't coming to Britain because Ryman's opened a branch in Streatham.

'This is nonsense and we should argue that statistically this is not true. If it were true then Britain would have 26 million people here already – that is three times the population of London. And no one in Leeds or Harrogate can argue that 26 million people have suddenly appeared on the basis that they heard a Polish accent in the garden centre.'

'NO!' bellows Tracey in her broad Welsh Valleys accent, 'I won't use logic on these bastards.'

So we wrote, 'Pull my finger'.

We spend the next hour or so wandering the Leeds ring road looking for posters and arguing

Photo: Tracey Moberly

what to put on them when we do find them. About 3 a.m. we walk along a near-deserted street, lit with a dull yellow glare, when we find another UKIP poster, a picture of the white cliffs of Dover and the slogan:

No border. No control.

'Right,' I begin, 'we have got to argue that this is scaremongering. What about the people who leave the UK to work in Europe? What about the controls on people outside the EU? There are 4 million non-British citizens working in the UK, paying National Insurance and tax into a Treasury that has seen receipts plummet. We have—'

'NO,' she bellows once more, her vowels echoing in the side streets, 'I won't even use words on these fuckers!'

'What shall we put?'

Slowly and menacingly she replies, 'A giant cock and balls.'

And so it was that at 3 a.m. in the morning, I am standing on a long lightweight aluminium ladder spraying a giant cock and balls in gold paint onto a UKIP poster when a police car draws level with me … and then drives past into the distance.

Never underestimate a hi-vis vest.

Photo: Tracey Moberly

While touring I start each show by asking for a member of the audience to take a plastic money bag (*for £1 coins*) and request that they take the bag in the interval, go outside the venue and fill the bag with soil. Each show started the second half with the collection of the small bag of soil.

Nigel Farage and his supporters are oft heard to utter the words, 'I want my country back.'

So I have been posting him bits of country back from every show.

He has had pot-plant soil, municipal soil, a vicar in Stowmarket even collected consecrated soil from his cemetery, all of which has been posted back to Nigel – over 200 bags' worth. It's not his country in its entirety, but it is a start and I hope he appreciates the gesture of ACT 52.

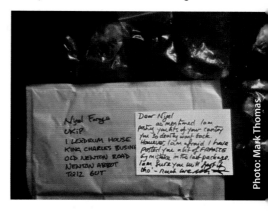

And to those of you who ask, 'Did you put a stamp on it?'

I reply thus: 'Do you think I'm a fucking amateur!'

———◆———

ACT 53 How does one pronounce that word 'farage'? It should sound like a good English word, *faraj*, as in, rhymes with garage. The pronunciation *fah radj* is nothing more than French affectation, and if Nigel wants to be called *fah radj* he should fuck off to France.

To reclaim the pronunciation and indeed a sense of Englishness about the word I took inspiration from the word 'santorum'.

Rick Santorum was an American senator and is currently campaigning for the Republican Party candidature for US President in the 2016 elections. After Santorum made a series of homophobic remarks equating gay sex with bestiality and paedophilia, the gay writer Dan Savage organised a competition to create a neologism for santorum. The winning definition was defined thus: 'santorum: the frothy mixture of lube and fecal matter that is sometimes the by-product of anal sex.'

The new definition has become so popular that it frequently appears in the top listings of various internet searches; to the extent that the ex-senator asked Google to remove the definition from their search engines. They declined.

Thus inspired, I thought, let us find a new definition for the word farage; let us create our own neologism. After all, the word, when pronounced correctly, has a wonderful British feel to it – you might expect it to crop up on *Countryfile* or *The Archers*:

Jack: Where have you been Fred?

Fred: Sorry, I've been laying down the farage and it took a bit longer than I expected. There's a lot more of it after the weather we've been having.

The objective is to find a suitable definition, use and promote it into common parlance, and if successful and the word does enter the vernacular, the eventual destination is the *Oxford English Dictionary*. So what I am saying is you might have to wait 20 years for the punchline to this.

I asked audiences and anyone who approached me to come up with suggestions for the definition of the word farage. These definitions were submitted online, via Twitter, indeed there was even a special website set up just to receive these definitions: www.nigelfarage.org.

No one in his team thought of buying that one.

Here is a list of some of the entries for the neologism competition:

farage (verb)
The passing of wind while performing a yoga position.
He went into a downward-facing dog pose and faraged loudly.

farage (verb)
Searching for un-findable dog excrement.
It was dark, she went in the bushes. I've faraged for an hour but, sod it, I've given up.

farage (verb)

The action of looking over your shoulder before saying something racist. Normally this is done twice over each shoulder before beginning a racist comment, often accompanied by the phrase, *I'm not a racialist but …*

farage (noun) (medical)

A tear between genitals and anus often occurring due to vigorous wiping.
The patient presented with a weeping farage, requiring stiches.

farage (noun)

The shape of a man's semi-erect penis in tight swimming trunks.
He hasn't been in the pool – look at the farage on him.

farage (verb)

A confused and angry wank.
I got home pissed and faraged over Newsnight.

As admirable as many of these suggestions may be, there can be only one winner. The winning definition to create a neologism for farage is:

farage (noun)

The liquid found at the bottom of a waste bin or container.
The bag for the food waste slipped and I've dripped farage all over my slippers.
Your neighbour should do something about his bins; they stink of farage.

I can think of no other word that describes this, other than bin-juice, but that is two words and why hyphenate when you have farage?

Although one can hyphenate when using farage when referring to the following:

1. Liquid in the salad crisper, *fridge-farage*.
2. Frozen farage, *farage-sicle*.
3. Farage spilt onto a shoe or slipper, *foot-farage*.

———————————✦———————————

ACT 54 was the creation and promotion of a sticker to help people with some of their farage issues.

And very popular it has proved too.

Photos of deployed stickers as tweeted by various audience members.

ACT 55 was commissioning a musical song explaining the neologism, and who better to write it than a musical duo that UKIP members tried to ban from various theatres – none other than Jonny & The Baptists. You can buy it online but here are the lyrics:

Uh-huh, you got it.
Drop the beat Nigel
Jonny & The Baptists here
We got ourselves some banging UK Farage

There was a brand new word around, and that word was the talk of the town
(Farage)
We didn't know what it might mean, but it's a nasty and unpleasant sound
(Farage)
We had to find out what it could be, was it a stench or a fungus or pissing yourself publicly?
This country's a democracy, so we had a vote to get it in the dictionary

Is it looking over one's shoulder before saying something racist?
(Farage)
Is it stoking public fears without any evidential basis?
(Farage)
Is it a smell that lingers in the air and the culprit can't be apprehended?
(Farage)

We searched the whole wide world
To find the true meaning of Farage
We trawled through a million words
To find the true meaning of Farage

It's pronounced Farage
It's spelt like it sounds
It rhymes with same-sex marriage
Let's spread it around
Like a nuclear spillage
It's an 'idge' not an 'arge'
It's an equality sandwich
Not a bigotry collage
Like post-colonial baggage
It just follows you around
Like an idiot in a village
There's always one to be found
Have you heard about Farage?
It's like ouzo and sick
That's the thing about Farage
It's onomatopoeic

Mmm. Yeah. What?
Yes. Hmm. Good. Mmm-hmm. More.
One Two Three Three Four. What?

Is it the scum that forms on top of your tea when you leave it to brew for too long?
(Farage)
To try and argue that your facts are right even after they've been proven wrong?
(Farage)
To try and justify a tedious link like flooding and gay marriage?
(Farage)
Just another term for shitting yourself, for example 'Nigel has faraged'?
(Farage)

Could it be the collective noun for a group of two or more pricks?
(Farage)
Just like you'd have a murder of crows, you'd have a Farage of dicks?
(Farage)
There are so many different things that we want this word to mean
(Farage)
But at the end of the day only one can reign supreme

From the whole wide world
Here comes the true meaning of Farage
Out of a million words
Here's the true meaning of Farage

Farage
It's the juice from your bin
Start using the word Farage
To describe the juice that lies within
Do you remember Farage?
It's what we used to call bin-juice
But now we have the word Farage
And it's time to set it loose
So watch out for the Farage
It smells like dysentery and gin
Keep away from the Farage
It's made of takeaway and sin
Gotta clean up that Farage
Let's start a new trend
Cause nobody wants Farage
So go tell all of your friends

Farage up.

ACT 56 was inspired by UKIP – and not just in a negative way either, though that is implicit – as I actually admire the way they communicate directly to their target voters through advertising.

Inspired by UKIP I decided to take a leaf out of their book and take out my own advert, hoping to emulate their direct marketing style. The advert is an invitation to Romanians to come and work in the UK, written in Romanian and published in the Romanian press. It started:

Dear Romanians,

COME TO BRITAIN!

It is fabulous here and I am sure you will like it.

Yes we have some foaming at the mouth rabid racist politicians but we regard them as sources of entertainment rather than fear, come and enjoy their stupidity with us.

All the best,
Mark

———————◆———————

ACTS 57-64

TAXES, TAXIS & TRADEMARKS

In the summer of 2013 I was approached by Theatre Uncut, a political theatre group who get well-known writers to create short plays around a political theme. I would say they commission these plays, but no money changes hands. The plays are made available online to perform without licence or copyright for a period of a month. The plays become the starting point for a truly international festival of political theatre and they are performed across the world by professional actors, teachers, am-dram types, students and strikers.

Theatre Uncut said to me, 'Mark we have enough clever people writing for us, will you contribute something?'

'I am your man,' I said with the certainty and ability of H. Simpson, and set about ACT 57.

During the Edinburgh festival, where I was performing, I spent late nights bashing out a script. The result is my play:

CHURCH FORCED TO PUT UP GATES AFTER FONT IS USED AS WASH BASIN BY MIGRANTS

If you think the title of the play is crap don't blame me, blame the actual *Daily Express* headline it was taken from.

To my immense delight it has been performed by a number of student groups and ended up performed at the Young Vic theatre as part of the Theatre Uncut season.

The play is about a right-wing newspaper owner *(oxymoron alert)* who is taken hostage by the cleaners, who demand he publish a pro-immigration editorial. It was written to promote three points:

1. There are 3 million foreign nationals employed in the UK, making up 10% of the workforce – working and paying taxes.

2. The *Daily Express* (proprietor Richard Desmond) is the most anti-immigrant newspaper in the UK and constantly attacks migrants and the unemployed. The company that owns the *Daily Express* has multiple off-shore entities. So the company that moans loudest about scrounging is not averse to not paying in to the pot in the first place.

3. I wanted to promote **ACT 58**, a demonstration outside the *Daily Express* headquarters demanding the *Daily Express* stop sponging off of immigrants!

Barely a breeze blows on this light balmy evening, and imagine if you will a small crowd gathering on the pavement in shorts and summer attire outside the *Daily Express* building. A few police keep their distance and liaise with the company's security staff. The Green Party London mayoral candidate has turned up to give support, as well as friends, people fighting campaigns for immigrants' rights and my chum Chris Coltrane, who happily hoists his banner high. It's a photo of Princess Diana and the slogan, 'Let's be honest, Princess Diana would have hated tax dodging!'

Add to this vision half-a-dozen journalists leaving the building,

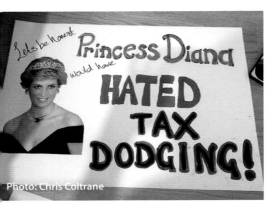

Photo: Chris Coltrane

looking various shades of worried to concerned, and you have a pretty good picture of **ACT 58**, the demonstration outside the *Daily Express* building.

I tried to hire a Princess Diana lookalike; the aim was to walk into the *Daily Express* newsroom shouting, 'I've found her! Stop the conspiracy theories! I've found her. In Tenerife! Hostess in a bar.'

That was the plan, but every time I approached a Princess Diana impersonator they said no.

———————◆———————

Indeed my failure to find a willing Di-a-likey was not the only time things went wrong, and not every idea worked in its initial form. I submitted a motion for a petition to the government's direct.gov.uk website – a scheme whereby, if your petition is accepted and gathers enough support and signatures, it forces a debate in the House of Commons.

The petition I submitted was:

> The government is to introduce a bill to regard any public statements by city bankers or hedge fund managers to the effect that 'they will leave the country if they do not get their bonuses' as a legally binding verbal contract.

They rejected it. I failed. And in the white heat of shame I was moved to create my own website for **ACT 59**:

WWW.WE WILL DRIVE THEM TO THE AIRPORT.CO.UK

I began building a volunteer taxi army to drive the bankers, energy bosses and any other grasping cad to the airport. Visit the site, sign up, become a volunteer driver. Then next time one of them begins their predictable mewling, we will pick them up, drive them to the airport, they can fuck off to Dubai and Jim Davidson can meet them at the airport.

We have over a thousand drivers and when you join you can, if you choose, set up your own profile page on the site, displaying a photo of your vehicle and in a special features section you may detail the route, in-car entertainment and refreshments you might provide for the bankers. There is a Driver of the Week certificate issued to drivers with the most commitment and flair. The first driver of the week was a biker called Woody, whose SPECIAL FEATURE simply read:

I'm a bit handsy

The second volunteered with a small cannon and pledged he would get them to their seat even if they were a bit late and the gate had closed.

The third simply said:

I'm blind but for these fuckers I'll give it a go

You are now leaving the UK

(for tax purposes)

BOOK YOUR VOLUNTEER  ONLINE

ACT 60 A letter to the Chancellor, George Osborne, sent May 2014:

Dear Chancellor,

I want to help you reintroduce the 50p tax rate.

You and your kind have oft said that if the rate of tax goes up the rich will leave the country (though many of them financially left for Jersey or the Caymans long ago), indeed the same reason is given for not curbing bankers bonuses; if they don't get paid obscene amounts of money they will simply up sticks and go. Problematically you have offered no hard evidence that this actually happens, just the periodical sabre-rattling from the CBI or IOD.

All of that changes now.

I am organising a national network of volunteers ready at a moment's notice to drive bankers and any number of assorted rich oiks to the airport should they choose to make good on their threats to leave the UK. If they would leave the country for money it stands to reason they would not turn down a free taxi ride. It is also a marvellous example of David Cameron's 'big society': people working together for the common good. A bit like Gary Barlow's charity work except without the tax dodging.

So I am in a unique position to tell you exactly how many bankers have left the country or indeed how many will leave, as I will be organising their transport to the airport.

So far none have gone. Absolutely none. Not one.

So I reckon the 50p tax rate can be slammed on straight away and think of all the marvellous things you could fund with that money: hospitals, schools, even scrap the bedroom tax. You might even consider funding HMRC to chase a few more celebrity donors to the Tory party for their tax-dodging antics.

If one single banker leaves I will let you know and we can throw the anchors on the whole shebang. I have a loud klaxon and a flare gun, which I am happy to sound and fire if a banker does head for the airport, in which case you can reverse the 50p tax rate pronto and probably stop them before they get on the plane.

Yours sincerely,

Mark Thomas

PS Please do not regard this a charitable activity that should be rewarded with an OBE or indeed any kind of honour, it is enough to know that I have helped.

More than one Act had a starting point in a show I have done since 2009 called the *Manifesto*, which occasionally pops up on BBC Radio 4; the audience is invited to submit their policies to change the world. Each night I discuss these proposals with the audience and they vote on their favourite policy.

Some policies voted by the audience:

Bristol – *To burn David Cameron in a wicker man to ensure a good harvest.*

Edinburgh – *All strike action should have a money-back guarantee (so if the strikers lost they would get the money they would have earned had they gone into work).*

London – *All models should be chosen at random from the electoral register. Future models to be informed of their assignment in the same manner people are informed of jury service.*

Cardiff – *Anyone found guilty of a homophobic hate crime should serve their entire sentence in drag.*

London – *All cashpoint machines should have a gamble button.*

London – *To create a 'bastard trade' logo, similar to the Fairtrade logo but with less emphasis on corporate 'good works'.*

The last policy not only won the vote but also was broadcast on BBC Radio 4. As was an amendment to the policy:

'That the logo of "bastard trade" should be a picture of a businessman punching an African child in the face.'

To ignore an idea like this would be a sin, so for **ACT 61** Greg the designer and I set about creating the logo.
  The result was so offensive I issued a fatwa on it.
  'We need an image that is less abrasive to people's sensibilities,' I say.
  'OK,' Greg says, 'I completely understand.'

This was what he came up with instead:

'Seriously?' I said to Greg, 'A man pissing on a boy. Seriously? Do you want to end up in the 70s' Entertainers' wing of Ford Open?'

'I'll try again,' he said.

So this is the image Greg and I compromised on; this is the official Bastard Trade logo.

At this point my long-suffering and oddly long-term researcher Susan said to me, 'That's not being as inventive and challenging as it could be, is it?'

'Oh,' I said in a tone best used by the King of Umbrage, 'what do you suggest?'

'Why don't we see if we can trademark the Bastard Trade logo?'

'Can we?'

'We can try.'

'Because then it would become the officially recognised international symbol of bad corporate behaviour.'

We hurriedly found the Intellectual Property Office website to search for the procedure to trademark a logo. My face drops in dismay as it becomes clear we cannot.

'You can't trademark words in common usage,' says Susan reading from the computer. 'The word "bastard" and the word "trade" are words in common usage and therefore you cannot trademark them.'

'That is frustrating.'

'It makes sense,' she continues. 'No one should own a word like "bastard". If someone had the rights to "bastard", they would make a fortune every time David Starkey appeared on TV.'

'We have failed,' I say, slumping in silence and staring into space dismayed and disgruntled.

After a pause Susan says, 'Not necessarily …'

'Really?'

'We can't copyright the word "bastard" and we can't copyright the word "trade" but we could try joining the two words together. Bastardtrade, like Fairtrade. Thus making a word hitherto unused, creating a unique word and logo and possibly subject to copyright law.'

So we applied to the IPO to copyright the BastardTrade logo.

And on **29 May 2013** the BastardTrade® logo became the internationally recognised symbol for shit corporate behaviour: ACT 62.

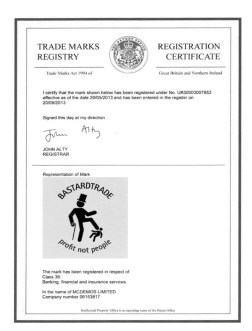

I printed shitloads of stickers and gave them away at gigs. In return I got hundreds of pictures and emails tweeted back of the logo deployed.

So great was the response that we decided to inaugurate the very first annual BastardTrade® award: ACT 63.

With a team of judges – *Ethical Consumer* magazine director Tim Hunt, War on Want executive director John Hilary, NUJ general secretary Michelle Stanistreet, and Hilary Jones, ethics director at Lush cosmetics company – we whittled down the shortlist to three:

RBS
G4S
Coca-Cola

You can vote on who wins the BastardTrade® award and find out more about the nominees by going to: www.markthomasinfo.co.uk to cast your vote.

The winner will receive this glorious trophy and get the right to display the BastardTrade® logo on their products.

Photos of deployed stickers as tweeted by audience members.

Although not included in the final nominees Gap still warranted some BastardTrade® attention for its refusal to sign The Bangladesh Accord on Fire and Building Safety, a code of practice created with garment workers to try and prevent incidents like the Rana Plaza building collapse that killed 1,129 people. A host of companies signed up to it, from Primark to Marks and Spencer. Gap was conspicuous by its absence, despite working in nearly 80 factories in Bangladesh. ACT 64 saw me join War on Want protestors outside a Gap store in Knightsbridge.

Photo: iDJ Photography

ACTS 65-68

DIPLOMACY, DANCING & DATA PROTECTION

ACT 65 was the second Act inspired by the *Manifesto*, and specifically a gig I did in Belfast where the audience voted for two ideas to be joint favourites:

1. Make it illegal for people to walk about the streets in their pyjamas.

2. To introduce the Abortion Act 1967 to Northern Ireland.

There isn't that much difference between the religious intolerance of Ireland and the religious intolerance of Northern Ireland when it comes to women's right to sexual and reproductive health. Basically if you are a working-class Northern Irish woman and you have an unwanted pregnancy you'd better borrow the fare to London and the clinic or start drinking heavily.

In 2014, working with the Alliance for Choice and the Northern Ireland Family Planning Association we organised a pro-choice comedy benefit in Northern Ireland, featuring Bridget Christie, Robin Ince, Josie Long and Gemma Hutton.

———————◆———————

ACT 66 was another piece of cultural dissent, albeit rather more guerrilla in fashion: I organised a free pro-gay stand-up comedy gig in the street outside the Russian consulate.

The Russian authorities are not noted for their liberal attitude to sexuality, or indeed anything that deviates from the deification of Putin, Mother Russia and God.

Gay Pride in Russia is an event noted for the assaults upon the LGBT community, which at best occur with the tacit consent of the police.

Indeed Russia has introduced a new law that prohibits transsexuals, transvestites and others from driving. If any transactivists want to borrow a remote-controlled Barbie car I am happy to help.

During the Edinburgh festival, working with the Equality Network and Stonewall, we organised the outdoor show, featuring gay, lesbian and bisexual comics, and myself representing overweight heterosexual fathers. We publicised the show on Twitter and by email.

Days before the show a very pleasant police officer contacted me, unannounced, and informed me there was a safety issue with the show.

'If 100 people turn up outside the Russian consulate they will move from the pavement into the road,' he said.

'Oh.'

'We're estimating at least 500 people turning up.'

'Oh dear.'

He informed me that by law I should request permission to shut the street from Edinburgh city council.

'But,' he added, 'that's a very bureaucratic process and you will spend all day on the phone, filling out forms and you will end up tearing your hair out ... The best thing,' his voice lowered in confidential tones, 'is don't bother with any of that and tomorrow afternoon when you start the event I'll take the spontaneous decision to shut the street with a couple of vans at each end.'

Somewhat taken aback, I spluttered, 'You're planning to take a spontaneous decision tomorrow?'

'I am indeed,' he laughed. 'It's best all around.'

So without fuss the street was shut. Six hundred people turned up; gays, lesbians, bis, trans, visitors, people who lived in the area, people who worked in the area, festival goers, festival performers and my friend Roy *(a pervert and a member of the Sisters of Perpetual Indulgence).*

Photo: Howard Binysh

The speakers, amp and mic were powered by bicycle-powered generator, ridden by a crack team of crusties, trans and lesbians.

Chris Coltrane, Joe Lycett, Stephen K. Amos, Susan Calman and Zoe Lyons all did a stint.

Performing on an impromptu stage/soapbox and battling with the mic's short lead, Chris proclaims, 'Putin wants to stamp out gays, well he should stop posing in photos like this.'

He holds up a large picture of a topless Putin in combat trousers.

'I believe Putin is conflicted,' Chris continues, 'which is why I would like to make this formal offer to the Russian consulate: I will take one for the team and fuck Putin so he can resolve his issues one way or another.'

Photo: Rob Hoon

Photo: Rob Hoon

Photo: Alan Gardner

Some Acts are silly; there is no getting round it, no dressing it up as situationism or a theatrical intervention. This is one of them. Tracey and I decided we would go into the West End stores in London, go to the customer toilets and on the back of the cubicle doors we would place stickers – not visible until you are in and the door shut. We imagined people in Liberty's and Selfridges *(were we able to get past security)* going to the loo, shutting the door, sitting down and looking up only to see the words '24-Hour CCTV in operation'. I will be the first to admit that ACT 67 is very childish.

In Liberty's – home of the hand-crafted overpriced scarf – I calmly move upstairs, enter the toilet, head straight to the cubicle, shut the door and retrieve the sticker and attach it to the door. On exiting the cubicle I see this sign on the wall:

CCTV is in operation in these toilets for the protection of staff and customers and the detection of crime

LIBERTY

The bastards are filming in the bog already! Seriously.

Two days later I head back to Liberty's, head up the oak staircase, along the wooden railings through the faux medieval/William Morris decor and to the public toilets with the CCTV sign in it. I stare into the dark blob of plastic hanging from the ceiling that conceals the camera and start to play a funk song in my mind, part funk part porn, full of chopping guitar riffs and lots of bass and brass.

I mouth the line, 'Come on.'

My hips start to move.

The guitar part cuts a rhythm, chopping a beat.

I drop to the beat, torso swaying as I sashay past the urinals.

The horn section blasts its arrival.

My head bobs and nods in time, leading my body as I lurch forwards.

My feet start to shuffle.

'Yeah!'

My arms tuck in tight then suddenly they are flung out and I flail in a circle twisting and dipping.

The horns pick up the hook and grind with drummer.

I shimmy to the cubicles, turning on one foot by the doors, leaning against them. My leg tucks up coquettishly and I start to reach up to the top button of my shirt. Undoing it to the song. Hands slipping down the other buttons, my fingers running through my chest hairs and soon the shirt is slipping from my shoulders. Slowly at first, lingering, waiting, then a dramatic rip and fling of fabric to the floor.

'That's right! Yeah!' I mutter.

Automatically, I am feeling for the belt, hurriedly grasping the tapered end, wrenching it against the buckle and drawing it through the loops.

'Yeah!' I sing and howl.

Amid a pile of shirt and trousers, I'm dancing in my Y-fronts. Winding my backside, pouting and slapping my cheeks, twisting in the mirror, all the while holding my own gaze.

Then it is over. I dress quickly. Head out of the toilets, into the store as the sunlight begins to drift through the glass ceiling. Before I know where I am I'm handing one of the Liberty's managers a letter, requesting all the video footage they have of me under the Data Protection Act: ACT 68.

Liberty's complied with the request, sending photos and video footage; there is even a short film of me entering the toilets. However, the CCTV cameras were not recording in the toilet, so they were unable to send me that particular piece of cinematic pleasure.

Shame. I am sure many of you would want to see a 50-year-old fat dad strip in a public toilet.

Fortunately I did take a video camera in with me and put it by the sink.

Enjoy.

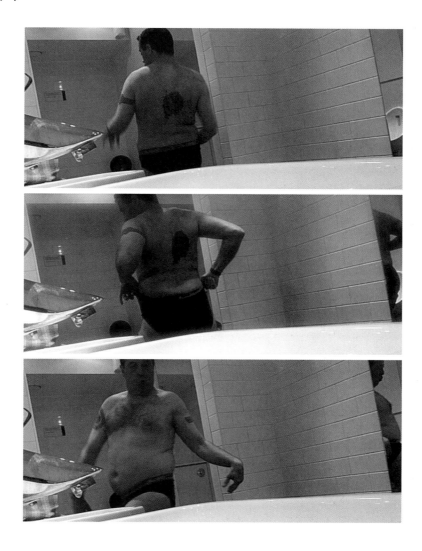

ACTS 69-75

BUSKING, BLACKLISTS & BALL GAMES

The London Borough of Camden is known for its music. From the Jazz Cafe to Koko to The Dublin Castle, it has a plethora of venues, not to mention Camden Market. It is a well-known law of physics that where spiked wrist bands and Ramones T-shirts are sold there will be buskers in the vicinity; their relationship akin to the Egyptian plover bird and a crocodile's teeth.

The local council do not have that same relationship with buskers, and using the Anti-social Behaviour, Crime and Policing Act 2014 they are introducing a licensing system for buskers in the borough. The licence, costing up to £47, comes with legal enforcement, and from **14 March 2014** busking without a licence in Camden exposes the musician to a potential £1,000 fine. Moreover the musician's equipment and musical instruments can be confiscated and SOLD, then used to offset the fine. Not only does this appear a tad draconian but buskers follow a basic rule – either get good and eat, or die hungry and tuneless.

At the invitation of comic and occasional Green Party candidate Ben Van der Velde and busking campaigner Jonny Walker, we set up the Citizens' Kazoo Orchestra (CKO), believing that should the police and the courts be able to find and profit from a second-hand market in kazoos, good fucking luck to them.

The CKO is an inclusive, radical and open orchestra. Anyone can turn up and play, they don't even need an instrument as we will probably have some spares. The first open rehearsal, ACT 69, is held outside Camden Tube station in North London. About 30 of us attend and start tentatively on 'Yellow Submarine'. A small crowd forms – it is Camden so frankly people gather to watch pigeons eat chips – and the open rehearsal veers into

Photo: Tracey Moberly Archive

STREET CULTURE IN CAMDEN IS UNDER SERIOUS THREAT

Camden Borough Council are planning to introduce one of the most restrictive Busking Laws in the UK.

- **Busking without a license will become a CRIMINAL OFFENCE** punishable by a fine of up to £1000

- Police, Council officials and *'authorised'* private contractors will have the power to **seize and confiscate instruments** of anybody busking without a license

- If fines are not paid within 28 days then the Council **can SELL the instruments** to pay the fine

- **All wind and percussion instruments and amplifiers are BANNED** *(including Kazoos)*

- **Annual licenses costing up to £123 will be required** with performers required to display licenses at all times and to **stop performing** if asked by a council official for any reason

GRAB A KAZOO AND JOIN THE DISSENTERS

MARK THOMAS 100 ACTS Of MIN@R DiSSenT

The **Citizens Kazoo Orchestra** has been formed by *Mark Thomas 100 Acts of Minor Dissent* in conjunction with the **Keep Streets Live** campaign.

Kazoos are highly portable and cheaper to replace than a guitar or violin should they be confiscated by an over-zealous public official.

We're open to new members *(with no previous Kazoo experience necessary)* and will be performing at events in Camden during the coming months.

Sign the online petition at www.keepstreetslive.com

Find out more at **www.facebook.com/groups/keepstreetslivecamden**

@designbyGreg

the kind of chaos that even proponents of the most obscure free-form jazz would object to. One section of the orchestra sticks with 'Yellow Submarine', another lurches into 'Abide with Me', a third breakaway group extemporise Jimi Hendrix solos and two drunks start singing 'You Belong to Me' in the corner.

———————————◆———————————

We managed a short practice for our next open rehearsal, ACT 70, and we invited Billy Bragg, Bill Bailey and the press. A small sea of people greeted us, kazoos held aloft, applauding as Bill Bailey sang his Billy Bragg parody 'Unisex Chip Shop'. Billy Bragg, looking on in mock outrage, provided rhythm guitar softly in the background, and I photographed a police officer. One brief moment of police intimidation evaporated as the crowd played 'Jerusalem' and 'Abide with Me' at the officers. The pathos of which would make Welsh male voice choirs weep.

After the new law was introduced, requiring £47 to play a kazoo, it looked as if the CKO was finished. However, Camden Council clearly states that traditional seasonal festivities, for example Christmas carol singing, processions and parades, and entertainment as part of a wider event, do not need a busking licence.

Photo: Tracey Moberly Archive

So we formed the Church of the Holy Kazoo: ACT 71.

Can I get a hallelujah?

The Church of the Holy Kazoo worships in the urban pathways of our capital, believing that those who have strayed from the path of righteousness and most in need of our ministrations are to be found on the streets of Camden. We worship by Camden Tube station and all of our hymns are played on the kazoo.

Why the kazoo? Out of respect for the scriptures, Psalms 150:6 tell us, 'Let everything that has breath praise the Lord'. Everything my friends, everything.

We at the Church of the Holy Kazoo can think of no better thing that embodies the scriptures' command than a kazoo.

Camden Council is welcome to challenge us for playing hymns on a kazoo outside the tube on a Sunday.

Photo: Rikki Blue

My name crops up on another list. Not only am I a domestic extremist but I am also a threat to the construction industry, and not merely because the extent of my DIY skills runs to switching on the telly manually without the remote.

It was an old comrade from the GMB* trade union who alerted me.

'We've got some of the names on the construction blacklist,' he said.

'Wow ...'

'And you're on it.'

'Fuck off ... really?'

'As one of the environmental campaigners.'

The construction blacklist was an illegal blacklisting scheme that mainly targeted trade unionists in the construction industry, workers who raised concerns over health and safety, and a smattering of activists. It was run by a company called The Consulting Association and was used to illegally deny workers employment; it was paid for and used by some familiar names:

Balfour Beatty
Carillion
Costain
Kier
Laing O'Rourke
Sir Robert McAlpine
Skanska UK
Vinci Plc
... and 36 others.

All have admitted their involvement and some workers have been offered compensation as low as £4,000. Considering the number of years some had been denied work, it is not surprising they rejected the offers.

---

* *General, Municipal, Boilermakers and Allied Trade Union.*

The Information Commissioner's Office confirmed in 2013 that my name appears on the list. I joined the GMB legal action with workers and activists against the blacklisting companies, **ACT 72**, and the day of action against the blacklist, **ACT 73**. The photo is outside McAlpine's office in Leeds with UCATT* members and, no, I did not grow the moustache to look like a late 70s' Trotskyist.

Several people contacted me on hearing the story to express their disappointment; apparently they were about to ask me to do their patio. I did used to work for my dad, a self-employed builder, and had he found out I was blacklisted he'd have said, 'Probably best all round, aye, love.'

———————◆———————

In all, there are four legal actions in the 100 Acts, and let me swiftly clarify that none of them have been brought *against* me:

The NUJ legal challenge to the police – **ACT 13**.

The GMB legal challenge to the blacklisters – **ACT 72**.

A failed attempt to overturn Camden's anti-busking laws, in conjunction with **ACTS 69–71**.

… and the fourth legal action, an intriguing case involving the minister for Culture, Media and Sport, the Royal Parks, an MP, one kilo of cocaine

---

* *Union of Construction, Allied Trades and Technicians.*

and a vibrating badger. Admittedly some of that is not true. I misspoke about the badger. And the MP ... OK and the cocaine. But the rest is true.

A year after the London Olympics, Hyde Park decided it would help deliver the Olympic legacy by introducing charges to play sport in parts of the park using a private company, Will to Win, to administer the scheme.

One of the first groups this affected was the London Charity Softball League, a whole bunch of people from NGOs like Amnesty and Save the Children who play softball against each other. So the first people the park pissed off were a large group of professional campaigners. Good work Park guys!

The softball players immediately organised an online petition, alerted the press and took part in ACT 74.

Any sport with a championship or league structure would now be subject to charges, so to test the resolve of Will to Win we organised the world's first 'What's the Time, Mr Wolf?' championship.

Around 100 people and 20 teams turned up for the game, as did a representative from Will to Win, who made an appearance, saw what was going on and quickly disappeared.

WHAT'S THE TIME MR WOLF?

1. The chosen 'wolf' stands at the far end of the field.
2. Players all shout the question, 'What's the time, Mr Wolf?'
3. With his or her back to the other players, the wolf calls out a time. For example, 'It's ... 6 o'clock.'
4. Players all take this number of steps forward.
5. Repeat numbers 2 to 5, getting closer to the wolf.
6. When close enough, instead of calling a time, the wolf can shout, 'It's ... DINNER TIME!!'
7. The wolf then chases the closest/slowest player.
8. Whoever gets 'tagged' becomes the next wolf.

Photo: Dan Mudford

I was umpiring, which explains the wolf onesie. The winning team was the Fuming Unicorns.

Photo: Vanessa Furey

For **ACT 75** we met again in the park for the world's first 'Stuck in Mud' championships. If truth be told, it was similar to **ACT 74** but with more bruises and dirt.

As for the legal challenge, well I know a lot of lawyers and was happy to play matchmaker. The London Charity Softball League, backed by Leigh Day, served legal papers on the Park and, on **20 March 2015**, following a consultation, the Royal Parks decided not to charge those playing sport in Hyde Park.

ACTS 76-80

DODGY LODGERS

The Apple Store on Regent Street most definitely stands in Regent Street, London, England, unlike its profits, which appear to be located somewhere in Ireland for tax purposes. But rather than dwell on the negative I thought, 'Let's celebrate Apple's Irishness!'

A group of us meet in John Lewis's coffee shop on Oxford Street, which is where we always meet when we are planning the downfall of international capitalism. Comfy sofas, free Wi-Fi and nice cakes – there's no need to make the overthrow of a world order unpleasant. We rehearse our action, leave and head to Apple, though we do return later with green charity tokens.

I shall leave the telling of **ACT 76** to Apple, as **ACT 77** was a DPA Subject Access Request to the company and they responded with this description of events:

From: ▮▮▮▮▮▮▮▮▮▮▮▮▮▮
Date: 3 June 2013 19:18:51 BST
To: ▮▮▮▮▮▮▮▮▮▮▮
CC: ▮▮▮▮▮▮▮▮▮▮▮▮

Subject: Protest at Apple Regent Street.

Hi,

We have just had a musical protest in the store around our taxation payments etc. A group of around 25 people entered the store just before 7pm and got changed into Irish costumes with flags and banners before playing music on instruments and dancing on the shop floor and stairs. The protest was lead by 'Comedian' Mark Thomas and lasted approximately 7 minutes. ▮▮▮▮▮▮▮▮ and the RZ managers approached the group and Mark Thomas asking them to desist as they were disrupting our customers and causing H&S issue by blocking the stairs. They were also filming.

We stated we would be calling the police as a precaution and they finished within a minute and left the store. They stood outside the store and photographed themselves before leaving the area.

This is already circulating on social media.

I have attached photos of the flyers they left in store.

That is their version, here is mine:

We did enter with banners proclaiming …

YOU ARE NOW ENTERING IRISH TERRITORY (FOR TAX PURPOSES)

… and then things became a tad chaotic, in part due to the delightful ceilidh fiddle band accompanying us who started to play the 'Irish Rover'. We handed out song sheets. The customers began to sing along, thinking us in-store entertainment. Riverdance broke out by the headphones. We merrily handed out leaflets.

At the planning meeting it was agreed when in-store security intervened they should be directed to the organiser. Sure enough I'm quickly surrounded and asked to leave, but while security gathers around me others are free to go to the display computers laid out on the shop's tables, put in a website address into the web pages and watch the store's own computers light up with the words:

**You can buy the SAME products
at the SAME price
at John Lewis around the corner
and their MD slams tax avoidance**

Unaware this is occurring, the store manager approaches me and says, 'If you don't leave I will call the police.'

'Considering your company pay nothing for their upkeep that's a tad ironic.'

We exit amid applause.

The following day I appear on a Boston radio station. The interviewer at one point asks, 'So how effective was your action? Do you think it reached many people?'

'Well, I'm talking to you in Boston.'

Photo: Tiernan Douieb

Apple is by no means the only culprit. It is one of many corporations that seem to have forgotten one crucial notion: profit is what you are taxed on, it is not what you make avoiding tax.

Take a glance at what remains of our high street and what you will see are the brands and logos of the companies that have forgotten this. Now these companies do all they can to avoid tax but they sure as hell want all the benefits that it pays for. They expect roads. They expect infrastructure. They expect public transport services to get their staff to work. They expect the emergency services if they have a fire or are robbed. They expect courts and jails to punish those who steal, assault or defraud them. They expect regulation and enforcement of the utilities they use. They expect their workers to be educated and healthy. They expect to be protected, nursed and nurtured. But are not prepared to pay their share of the bill. Frankly we can no longer afford to support these freeloaders.

ACTS 78-80 are gentle reminders to those companies that we expect them to pay their dues.

———————◆———————

Vodafone famously dodged its fair share of tax and cut deals with an over-malleable HMRC, so to remind them that we expect them to play a fuller part in our community I turned their shop in Bath into a community health noticeboard. In the early hours of the morning I plastered their shop front with genuine community health posters, so shoppers that morning would not only be able to purchase a phone package of texts, free minutes and data but would also learn how to check for bowel cancer: **ACT 78**.

Another early start sees friends and I arrive in Slough for **ACT 79**. In 2013 this was Amazon's head office in the UK, though its profits seemed to be appearing in the low-to-no-tax haven of Luxembourg. Making such a leap must be difficult for head office staff, moving from one fixed point in space to another in conceptual monetising.* So to help the staff we arrive early and take up positions by the entrances, smiling politely and offering chocolates and visas.

VISA   LUS 0123456X

VALID FOR / VALABLE POUR	LUXEMBOURG–UPON–SLOUGH		
FROM / DU	13-05-13	UNTIL / AU	14-05-14
NUMBER OF ENTRIES / NOMBRE D'ENTRIES	MULT	DURATION OF STAY / DUREE DE SEJOUR	1 YEAR
ISSUED IN / DELIVRE A	UNITED KINGDOM		
ON / LE	13-05-13		
TYPE OF VISA / TYPE DE VISA	TOURIST – FOR TAX PURPOSES		
REMARKS / REMARQUES	FULL RECOURSE TO PUBLIC FUNDS		

V C < L U S < < T E M P O R A R Y < < < < < < < < < < < < < < < < < < < <

N 0 0 0 1 2 3 4 5 6 G B R

Dear Amazon Staff and Workers

Greetings!

Would you please be so kind as to pass on to your employer this brief message:

Using Luxembourg to avoid paying tax in the UK is greedy.

Paying just £2.4m corporation tax despite UK sales of £4.2bn is rank at any time but in the middle of a recession it's selfish.

Paying less in corporation tax than you receive in government aid (the Scottish government paid £2.5m to expand Amazon's warehouse facilities) is taking the piss.

Thanks and enjoy the nibbles :-)

---

* I am not sure this is a thing.

Google use similar tax arrangements to Apple and Amazon: though they operate from the UK, the sales and payments go through Ireland. The company explained its low UK tax bill saying that although some of its sales work was done in the UK the actual *finishing* of the contracts happened in Ireland and was, therefore, naturally subject to the lower *Irish* tax rate. A state of affairs even MPs said was 'devious, calculated and … unethical'.

Photo: Rikki Blue

Just before staff arrive to their UK head office near Tottenham Court Road, I arrive with Danny Shine, a renowned one-man situationist public-address system, whose use of the loudhailer has turned him into a performance artist. If anyone knows how to communicate to the pedestrian rush hour it is Danny.

We stand a megaphone apiece each end of the public square by the office entrances. 'Please do not attempt to interact with Google staff today,' Danny bellows like a train announcer. 'Due to economic necessity their work must be finished in Ireland. Just to be on the safe side, do not finish any activity with Google staff in case it is a taxable activity. Do not finish conversations. Do not finish sentences. In fact, if you work for Google, don't even start a toilet break.'

For some reason the security for the building decide to shut all the entrances except one, thus making the staff queue to get in and having the unintended consequence of making our job somewhat easier.

'We should all thank Google for being so philanthropic,' the megaphones bellow. 'They insist that their staff don't complete their work tasks. How nice of the company. If only more companies would give their employees a lighter workload.'

We do this for an hour: **ACT 80**.

ACTS 81-87

ESTATE AGENTS: 'EVERYONE HATES YOU'

ACT 81 You do not need to be a genius to sell houses during a housing shortage, you just need to be a greedy twat. The failure to build social housing has seen the wholesale gentrification of large parts of London, so in an effort to stem the tide friends and I set up the Neighbourhood Welcoming Committee.

When estate agents have viewings for houses going for over a million we turn up to greet the prospective neighbours.

I shout, 'I like crack.'

Tony sings, 'Hello.'

Tracey just stands there and Dave says, 'Do you want a biscuit?'

And then we sing the theme from *Neighbours* at them.

Photo: Phil Stebbing

The estate agent appeared, looked at us and called the police, saying, 'One of them has a sign with "I heart crack" and they are standing outside my viewing.'

The police never came, the estate agent buggered off but one of the viewers shared some cider with Tony.

If you are looking for an image of pollution and provocation you could do worse than consider the estate agents' signs, especially ones with the word SOLD on them. These properties are sold; there is no need to advertise them. What that SOLD sign does is peddle fear; fear that you'd better hurry up and get that deposit down, fear that you'll never be able to afford this place, fear that the market has beaten you. And in this case it most probably has and is now just rubbing your nose into it.

Tracey and I decided to use the basic ingredients of this pollution to create messages for the estate agents and the gentrifiers.

ACT 82

ACT 84

ACT 86

ACT 87

ACTS 88-94

(IN)CONSIDERATION

During the Edinburgh festival every available room with a light switch is turned into a venue or a hostel, which is why I found myself performing in the police social club. It's a down-to-earth establishment and not subject to finicky modern requirements like disabled access. Unsurprisingly, a woman wrote to me about this issue: it was unfair to perform in a venue that many would find impossible to get into. She explained I had a choice, I could either find a venue with proper access or do a gig in her living room.

The living-room show was drunken, raucous and fun, packed with a disabled audience and their carers. Afterwards, sitting with a paper plate laden with baps, surrounded by whiskey and cake, the talk moved to the Work Capability Assessment (WCA) and Atos, the IT company brought in by the government to run it and 'assess' whether people with disabilities were fit for work.

The real and intense anger about this scheme was perhaps to be expected; there were after all many stories of Atos having targets, quotas of people to remove from the benefits system. What took me by surprise was the fear. Intelligent adults were afraid of the assessment; they talked of their anxiety and stress, and some were genuinely terrified of the consequences. They relayed awful tales of people bullied and abused by the assessors, made to wait in pain, often travelling long distances on public transport to a building that had no access for them.

What kind of cruel bureaucracy compels disabled people to attend an assessment centre with no disabled access? Is it incompetence? Bad judgement? Was it part of the assessment, a witch trial if you like: if they can enter the centre they're fit for work, if they can't they failed to attend and must be burnt at the stake.

The anecdotes in the living room were compelling and shocking. What people wanted was to be treated decently, with dignity and respect. What would happen, I mooted, if we turned the tables on Atos and assessed how they were doing? The room gave this thought a very positive reaction and was probably the best material I'd used all evening.

I was fortunate enough to come into contact with various disability rights groups and campaigners who were prepared to work with me, and together we devised a questionnaire, ACT 88:

ASSESSING THE ASSESSORS:
Are Atos Fit For Work?

The project was launched with a party outside Edinburgh's Atos assessment centre: ACT 89.

There would be time enough for demonstrations, outside the Atos head office in Triton square would be one of them; speaking at that demo became ACT 90. Bumping into campaigning group Black Triangle doing a guerrilla protest outside the BBC and being asked up to speak was another: ACT 91.

But for the time being our launch party had a relaxed and welcoming atmosphere – the antithesis of an Atos assessment – it was in fact an afternoon tea party, with hot beverages and glasses of squash, some comfy chairs, biscuits, cake and some close-up magic tricks performed by Ian Saville. If only all demos were this civilised. I've decided, come the revolution, I'm taking charge of the menus.

Photo: Mark Thomas

Then we set about getting the questionnaire distributed as far as possible, working as a network of groups passing information on to as many people as we could. Demos are fine, art interventions are great, protest is good, but there are times when you just need some good research, and that is what we set about doing.

Among the groups working on *Assessing the Assessors* was the WOWpetition, who had launched a petition on the government's website spearheaded by comic and writer Francesca Martinez.

The petition called for:

A Cumulative Impact Assessment of all cuts and changes affecting sick and disabled people, their families and carers, and a free vote on repeal of the Welfare Reform Act.

An immediate end to the Work Capability Assessment, as voted for by the British Medical Association.

In **November 2013**, 12 days before the petition was due to end, over 100,000 signatures had been collected, forcing the government to timetable a debate on the petition in Parliament.

Timetabling a debate on the impact of the cuts is one thing, getting MPs to attend is quite another. So for ACT 92 we created a map showing MPs how to physically get to the debate and emailed every MP in Parliament.

A HANDY GUIDE
to help prevent MPs getting lost
on their way to the WOW Debate

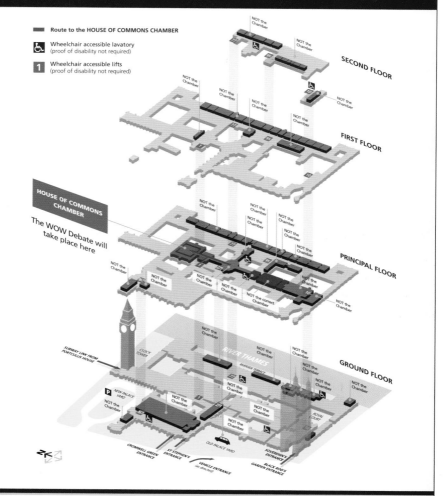

This helpful guide is brought to you by
@WOWpetition and **@100Acts**

Our questionnaire had by this point created 884 responses. And Dr Simon Duffy of The Centre for Welfare Reform kindly provided the academic expertise to evaluate the responses:

884 PEOPLE COMPLETED THE QUESTIONNAIRE

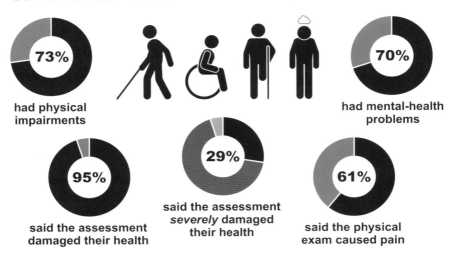

73% had physical impairments

70% had mental-health problems

95% said the assessment damaged their health

29% said the assessment *severely* damaged their health

61% said the physical exam caused pain

The report found the assessors and the centres completely unsuitable for the task. But perhaps the most disturbing was personal testimonies:

'The assessor watched me crawl across the floor to a chair, I was in tears of pain and humiliation.'

'There is an initial premise that you are a liar or fraud – it is abhorrent.'

'I went home crying, in fear that she would lie, and lo and behold she did. Now I have no Mobility Component, back to being housebound again at 19. What sort of life is this?'

'At the tribunal I was awarded 45 points, much, much more than the 6 points Atos gave me. The judge and GP there were lovely, understanding and actually listened to me and took my hospital notes into account. The judge, with tears in her eyes, apologised for my treatment by Atos and praised me for my determination and ability to cope.'

'She tutted and huffed throughout and asked, if I'd tried to commit suicide why I wasn't dead.'

'The computer system was down and I couldn't be interviewed. After over an hour waiting I was told to go home and await being sent for another interview. That night I suffered a heart attack and spent nearly two weeks in Papworth.'

'My benefits stopped on 19th Feb – not cut, stopped. For the first time in my life (55 years old) I have had to starve.'

We presented *Assessing the Assessors* as evidence to the House of Commons Parliamentary Select Committee. It was accepted and published in their report: ACT 93.

In **March 2014** Atos quit the WCA contract and received no compensation for the early termination of the work. But the assessments continue, just with a new company running them.

Read the report … If there is only one issue in these 100 Acts that would stir you to action, I hope it is this one:

 www.centreforwelfarereform.org/library/by-date/assessing-the-assessors.html

ACT 94. We produced these by the thousand, sold and gave them away. People used them and sent me the photographic evidence.
In **April 2014** a *Daily Mail* journalist, posing as unemployed and hungry,

Daily Mail Free Zone

Please show consideration for fellow passengers by not reading or leaving copies of the Daily Mail newspaper in this coach

approached a food bank run by the Trussell Trust. He was given a bag of groceries worth £40 and the *Mail* ran a major article criticising the Trust for not checking if people were really unemployed.

So I sell the poster of the collage opposite, and all profits go to the Trussell Trust. If you want to annoy the *Daily Mail* and help a food bank you can get the poster here:

 www.markthomasinfo.co.uk/section_store

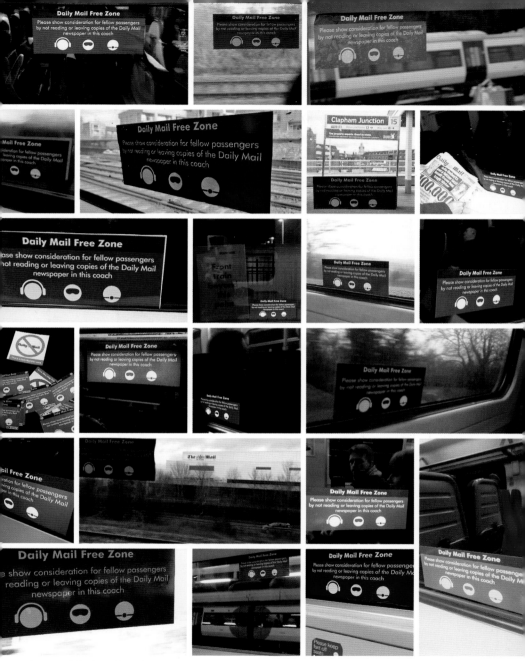

Photos of deployed stickers as tweeted by audience members.

ACTS 95-100

PORN & PIÑATA

An Act I do with my friend Tracey, the artist from the Valleys, is called the Pornershop.

Created as a reaction to my ambivalence to porn: namely the issue of censorship. Who has the right to tell adults what they may or may not do or watch? *(Naturally this comes with all the caveats of consent.)* If people want to look at pictures of themselves or other people fucking that is entirely up to them. What I do object to is when it appears in my local newsagents. I don't want my children growing up with those particular expectations of sex and sexuality to be considered as the norm.

This is how to Pornershop:

1. Walk into newsagents.
2. Select pack of porn in a cellophane wrap.
3. Pay for it.
4. Get home, carefully remove cellophane wrap, remove porn.
5. Cut, paste and collage each magazine.
6. Wait for glue to dry *(important part of process)*.
7. Insert porn magazines back into cellophane, resealing as if it has been unopened.
8. Return to newsagent of original purchase and surreptitiously place back on shelf.
9. Exit.

The first Pornershop action took place in Tooting Broadway, South London, because, well, frankly, I wasn't going to do the first one in my local shop. I envisaged walking into my local shop to buy the porn and they would say, 'No *Guardian* today, Mark?'

'Nah, I just fancied a wank,' I would reply, 'so thought I'd give this a go and if the cryptic crossword is any good, you know, make it a regular thing.'

So Tooting Broadway it was.

Boldly I pluck the first pack of porn from the top shelf, stride to the counter and declare, 'I would like to purchase these, my good fellow,' slapping the porn onto the Formica top. This is not the normal method of purchasing pornography, which usually involves some furtive glances at the very least.

The newsagent looks at me as if it say, 'This form of human interaction is unknown to me and yet I am sufficiently intrigued by it as to willingly enter into this puckish dialogue.'

He turns to me and equally bold proclaims, 'I would like to sell you these magazines.'

'That's a relief,' I say.

'Not in here.'

'Touché, monsieur.'

'Again,' he replies, 'not in here.'

He holds the barcode to the reader and says, 'That's £5.99.'

'Here are six of the Queen's good pounds.'

'Here is a penny of her change. Would you like a bag?'

'Yes please.'

It doesn't matter that the blue, thin plastic bag is see-through and the words 'OVER 50s' can clearly be seen through it; it is the thought that counts.

'Thank you.'

'No, thank you.'

Then he looks at me as if to say, 'That was fun but now it is time for you to leave as I have a gentleman adjacent to your very self eager to acquire HobNobs.'

Then, without thinking and slightly peeved, I say, 'Can I have a receipt please?'

A look of anger and contempt passes over his face as if to say, 'I have never given a receipt for pornography in my life. Do you think I accept returns? That someone might enter my establishment and say "Didn't work, I'd like a refund"?'

Due to the ferocity of his visage I blurt in explanation, 'It's so I can claim it against tax.'

But this only serves to inflame him more, his eyebrows raise and his mouth opens as he seems to recoil in horror, thinking, 'What kind of job do you have!?!'

'I am Ofwank,' I want to say, 'inspector of porn. Regulator of engorgement goods and services.'

But I don't.

Tracey and I open the porn on my kitchen table. It is a lot more graphic than I remembered it being when I would steal it as a teenager ... ah those summer balmy days we thought would last forever ... when the merest glimpse of hair in the genital area was as racy as it got.*

But how would we – indeed *could* we – subvert porn with our collages? After a long, coffee-fuelled discussion, ranging from Richard Hamilton to Jo Guest, we finally alight on the question of Margaret Thatcher's funeral and whether that had been some kind of establishment ideological deification/circle jerk of grief, in effect political pornography; it is then we decide on our first collage. We cut up hundreds of images of Thatcher heads from newspapers and magazines and paste them on to the models' bodies. The result is truly horrific and I apologise to everyone who has that image in their head – the image of a naked woman, standing legs slightly apart, back to the camera and Thatcher's head looking over her shoulder, the body language saying, 'Oh, hello, I didn't know you were there.' And a face that says, 'Gotcha!'

It is an image that few will forget nor forgive in a hurry. Though it is also inevitable that someone will roll back their eyes in delight, muttering, 'I have waited so long ... so long ...'

---

* For those of you born after the 1980s, we used to have a thing called pubic hair; our genitals back then were completely unwaxed and unplucked, completely lacking polish of any kind. Just hair.

For the second magazine in the batch we try an altogether less abrasive approach. Wally. We use Wally, the character from the kids' picture books in a red-and-white jumper and bobble hat. We cut out a host of Wallys from the kids' books, which is harder than it sounds because first you have to find him. Then we stick a Wally on every page of the porn.

Some of them are easy to spot – one emerges waving from the waistband of a pair of underwear – others require a modicum of study; we respect Wally's ethos. We have our happy-go-lucky popping out of a toaster, in a toothbrush mug, by the lamp stand and sticking out of a pile of cushions.

Tracey and I wonder if his presence will disturb, distract or delight those masturbating. They might, we reason, be Wally fans and get in the spirit of the work; some could – mid-strum as it were – catch sight of him and declaim, 'There's Wally!' and seek him out on every page. Others might spot Wally and

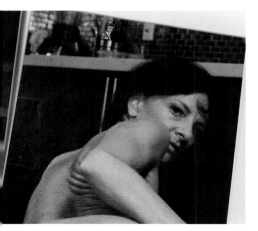

panic, wondering if their partner or kids had found their stash of porn and created a collage by way of confronting of them. Others still might experience alarm on sighting Wally, thinking, 'He's looking at me. Watching me doing what I'm doing. How much have you seen, you peeping bastard?!?!'

Then there is another reaction: that someone might find Wally and think, 'Oh I get it! This is a deconstruction of voyeurism. Wally's watching me, watching the models, who in turn return my gaze, aware they are being watched. This questions the "male gaze", while at the same time challenging my adult habits with a childish representation of innocence.'

Though the chances of that reaction are slim.

Two days later Tracey and I stride into the newsagent in Tooting Broadway with the doctored porn carefully placed back inside the packaging. Tracey goes to the counter to distract attention. I remove the porn from a rolled up newspaper, reach up and place the magazine on the shelf in the middle of the other porn, completing ACT 95.

On the way out I buy some gum and the shopkeeper says, 'Would you like a receipt for that, sir?'

Over the course of the next three Pornershop actions, Tracey and I have long arguments about the nature of what we are doing. Is this a genuine effort to subvert the porn or just spoiling an onanist's fun? Is it an art intervention or a schoolboy prank? I still don't know.

———————◆———————

ACT 96 Tracey's series of pen-and-ink drawings of the suffragettes Emmeline Pankhurst and Emily Davison, holding 'Votes for Women' banners, are attached to every page. The drawings are black and white, and attached to the porn is a set of drawing crayons. On the opening page we stick a statement: 'This is a special colour-and-keep edition of suffragette icons – please find attached crayon set.'

———————◆———————

162

ACT 97 The magazines that feature particularly young models we decide to treat as if they are a school kid's notebook and decorate them with stickers, rainbows, sparkles, stars, unicorns and cartoon characters. We also collage kittens, bunnies and puppies into the porn.

Ahh.

ACT 98 In the corner-shop porn we buy, the models seem to drop their kit and fuck everywhere but the bedroom, posing in kitchens, bathrooms and living rooms. In the background is the minutiae of our lives: fridges, coffee machines, washing-up bowls, shampoo and the like. I think it is an attempt to convince the viewer that what they are looking at is not contrived but somehow real – perhaps it is an attempt to distract from the artificiality. If I want to subvert and comment on commodification, why not use these images in the background. If this is about commodification, why not find all the background goods and put a price tag on them?

One picture features a woman naked and on her knees surrounded by five men standing wearing no trousers but all of them in T-shirts *(there is a line, a dignity, for everyone)*. We find a clothes catalogue with the same type of T-shirts for sale, cut out the prices and stick them on:

1. Grey Short-sleeve Polo
£12.99

2. Lemon Short-sleeve Polo
£12.99

3. Red V-neck T-shirt
£21.99

In another picture, with a man in his mid-fifties, in a shirt, having sex with a younger woman who is on all fours, we collage on:

Special Offer
4 SHIRTS
£25

The Pornershop is from the start an experiment, an exploration rather than a definitive statement. I simply do not know what we achieved, if anything. Jenny, my wife, and friends look at the magazines and their instant reaction is not what I expect. I doubt these words have ever been uttered by many people looking at porn – Jenny says, 'Fuck! That is expensive for a fridge.'

Tracey says we have created feminist art. My wife Jenny says we have created feminist art because, 'Tracey is an artist and Tracey is a feminist, and if she says it's feminist art then it is feminist art.' I don't know. All I know is that we are self-publishing a book of the images we created and the British Library has got 100 copies coming straight at them.

There is little time left to complete the final Acts, but the end is in sight and I am negotiating with the Sheffield Millennium Gallery over the art exhibition. I phone Greg the designer.

'We need to find a couple more Acts to finish the project.'

'I know,' he says, 'I have sent something for you over to the art gallery. It should be there when you turn up.'

It is.

And that lunchtime I send out a tweet:

Mark Thomas @markthomasinfo 7 May
I am in Sheffield Peace Gardens. I have a Nick Clegg
Pinata. Join me in an hour.

An hour later about 60 people – for the sake of argument, let's call them a mob – assemble in the city square, the very same square that Deputy Leader Nick Clegg filmed his May 2010 election video 'Say Goodbye to Broken Promises'. I produce the handmade Clegg piñata. It is Nick Clegg's *Simpsons* image; the more observant will have noticed his trousers are around his ankles and something protrudes from his bottom. Correct. It is the Coalition Agreement. Years from now when people ask, you will be able to say:

'Yes, as it happens I do know what happened to nuanced subtle satire: Mark Thomas killed it with rolled-up paper up the arse.'

Photos: Greg Matthews

Photo: Louise Jones

The crowd set about the piñata with the gusto and vim you would expect.

Finally the piñata is broken and the insides spill out, containing sweets and Lib Dem election pledges, broken ones obviously, and **ACT 99** is complete.

When assembling the art exhibition of 100 Acts in **May 2014**, Chris the technician asks me in a broad Sheffield accent, 'What to do wi' Clegg's body?'

'Suspend it from the ceiling in the middle of the room.'

'Right. Just torso?'

'Er, yes … er, don't know … what shall we do with the decapitated head?'

Chris smiles and says, 'I've stuck it on't spike.'

And so Clegg's head jutted into the air above the Millennium Gallery like a medieval blaggard.

Photo: Tracey Moberly

'You know what would be really good,' says Tracey, the artist from the Valleys, 'would be video screens around the gallery for people to interact with.'

We stand in the shell of the Millennium Gallery trying to visualise the exhibition of the 100 Acts.

'How many would be need?'

'Loads. I dunno. Ten. Twenty.'

'Where do we get them?'

'Dunno. Apple?'

ACT 100 is this letter to Apple:

Dear Sir/Madam

RE: Sponsorship

This is a request for sponsorship for an art exhibition in Sheffield titled Art of Dissent.

This is a unique chance to loan 10 Apple iPads to be displayed alongside artworks and play short films upon request.

One of the Acts of Minor Dissent for the show is a video of the flashmob in the Apple store in Regent Street London last year, featuring folk musicians and singers protesting Apple's tax structures that avoid a fair rate of UK taxation, so you are guaranteed a presence in the show regardless.

You can view the video here:
www.youtube.com/watch?v=n8gz4bE3Aqg

Were you to take up our generous offer to allow your products in our exhibition we believe it would be a very small act of contrition on your part. Though it is hoped that this might prove a first step for Apple, so one day the company might not regard itself above the commitments of ordinary people paying tax in the place they work.

Best wishes etc

The company replied:

Unfortunately, Apple does not offer any sponsorship opportunities at this time but we appreciate that you thought of us.

In honesty, I did not expect them to take up our offer and so instead I made these, to stick on their products when I pass them.

And, just for fun, **ACT 101**. I send UKIP a cheque for £1,000 from a bank account with no money in it.

———————✦———————

EPILOGUE

As a performer I am filled with an obsession, an eternal curiosity and fascination with … myself. Equally, I am baffled that others are not, so the following apology is frankly disingenuous: forgive me a moment of introspection.

In this year of dissent I loved waking up hearing my family cry in outrage 'Dad!' as they tried to find space for breakfast on a kitchen table covered in home-made banners that have been left to dry.

I loved turning up at the print shop to collect the posters of 'Estate agents: everyone hates you'.

I loved the printers saying, 'Nice.'

I loved my neighbours saying, 'Good work this morning,' after a new lot of posters went up.

I loved arriving at theatres and asking if there was any wallpaper paste in the building.

I loved that the theatre crew would giggle and help.

I loved the Dalmatian onesie more than I should have done.

I loved walking through Sheffield with the audience after the show, looking for the proposed new Curzon cinema, getting lost, finding it, and masses of us posing for selfies with the banners.

I loved the Curzon cinema workers winning and I cheered and cheered.

I loved meeting mates at 4 a.m. wearing overalls to do something bad.

I loved my lawyer laughing when reading my domestic extremist file.

I loved laughing at my fellow claimants' entries in their files.

I loved that the NUJ is with us on the court case.

I loved the pictures people sent of BastardTrade® stickers, of book-stickers, of farage stickers.

I loved someone at the *Red Pepper* office phoning to say, 'You can borrow my barge pole.'

I loved friends asking if they could bring a friend along to a demo.

I loved laughing with my postie on the doorstep when he told me how the local estate agents were pissed off with me.

I loved the *Daily Mail* stickers, I loved getting BastardTrade® trade-marked, I loved the ingenuity of people and their suggestions.

I loved playing in corporate space, on shelves, on posters, on playing fields, in streets in Camden, on a consulate doorstep.

I love that communities are not sealed in amber, nor set in stone, they are not fixed solely in advertisers' images of brass bands and cobblestones; communities are always in flux. They occur wherever we gather, online, at demonstrations, on playing fields, Tube carriages and for the duration of a show when a collection of individuals come together and become an audience, a group.

Despite my desire to create an audience and community, there is something peculiar in a performer's DNA. A thousand people could rise to their feet for a standing ovation at the end of a show and a performer will think, 'That bloke in the second row didn't, he hated the show from the start. I could see him with his arms folded all the way through.'

It is a trait we share with dictators.

There were 200 shows of the *100 Acts of Minor Dissent* but I want to tell you about Hull. Saturday night. October. Hull Truck Theatre. The gig is weird from the off.

I have not reached the mic to start the show when a woman shouts, 'I thought you were Mark Steel. You had better be good, because I love him.'

Then someone jumps onstage, mumbles something into the mic and takes a bow. Which is promptly followed by a short smiling drunk in a flat cap pointedly walking out in front of the stage from left to right in full view of the audience.

'You alright?' I ask.

'I am just going for some cheese,' he proclaims, exiting stage right.

This is the opening salvo in the battle that reaches a crescendo halfway through the first half when a young woman shouts from near a nest of drunks, 'Mark, will you sort this out please, they keep shoving me.' She is in a wheelchair. She is upset.

Twitter picks up the story …

'Absolutely right to lose your rag.'

'Was it a full moon tonight? Nutters galore at Hull Truck for Mark Thomas.'

'Were quality tonight pal, those you called cunts were absolute cunts and totally out of order! You dealt with it mint too.'

'Well done for superb crowd management. Reminded me too much of our teaching profession!'

'I've been going to HT years, never known an audience behave so badly.'

'Thanks for persevering. Car crash TV in parts uncomfortable to watch but you had to all the same.'

I speak to the young woman, Emma, after the show and it transpires the drunks had threatened her, calling her a hypochondriac.

'Are you going to report it?'

'Wasn't going to but maybe I should. I'm used to it.'

'Well perhaps you might think of calling the police.'

'I think maybe I should. One of them said, "I don't care if you're in a chair, I'll do you outside."'

The next day the local radio station run a special feature on my performance and they ask if I will appear on their show to defend myself, and it becomes apparent that the main issue they focus on, the one thing that really catches their presenter's attention, was that I called someone a cunt.

They didn't report that Emma did indeed call the police nor did they later report that one of the hecklers was later given a suspended sentence and fined for their part in the harassment.

One of the campaigners we worked with during 100 Acts told us that what he hated most about the benefits squeeze was how public opinion had changed towards disabled people. Campaigners had spent years trying to get some recognition and basic rights, only for it all to be snuffed out by the perception that disabled people were on the make, that they were lazy scroungers who were sucking the country dry. Never mind the 1,300 people who have died after being found fit to work by Atos, or the people living in fear of what the future holds. And while Atos has gone, the idea has not. Ian Duncan Smith and the Department for Work and Pensions have found a new company to administer their test – Maximus, a company who are willing to play with their reputation for the money thrown at them – but the test is the test no matter who administers it.

What I love, and I mean really love, is the ability we have to say, 'No.' To say, 'Nah, fuck it, not in my name. You cunts.'

———————◆———————

APPENDIX

HOW TO MAKE A SUBJECT ACCESS REQUEST* UNDER THE DATA PROTECTION ACT

[Your full address]
[Phone number]
[The date]

[Name and address of the organisation]

Dear Sir or Madam

SUBJECT ACCESS REQUEST

[Your full name and address and any other details to help identify you and the information you want.]

Please supply the information about me I am entitled to under the Data Protection Act 1998 relating to:

[give specific details of the information you want, for example:]

- your personnel file;
- emails between 'A' and 'B' (between 1/6/11 and 1/9/11);
- your medical records (between 2006 & 2009) held by Dr 'C' at 'D' hospital;
- CCTV camera situated at ('E' location) on 23/5/12 between 11am and 5pm;
- copies of statements (between 2006 & 2009) held in account number xxxxx.

If you need any more information from me, or a fee, please let me know as soon as possible.

It may be helpful for you to know that a request for information under the Data Protection Act 1998 should be responded to within 40 days.

If you do not normally deal with these requests, please pass this letter to your Data Protection Officer. If you need advice on dealing with this request, the Information Commissioner's Office can assist you and can be contacted on 0303 123 1113 or at ico.org.uk.

Yours faithfully
[Signature]

---

* Courtesy of the Information Commissioner's Office: www.ico.org.uk.

HOW TO MAKE YOUR OWN 'ARSEY COPS' DESK CALENDAR

Items you will need:
- A photocopier
- An empty CD jewel case
- An empty cereal box
- Glue or double-sided tape
- Some 'Calendar Tabs'
  (available from most craft shops)

Step 1:

Photocopy the following six pages using the 'A4 to A3 enlargement' setting *(it's OK, we won't sue you for breach of copyright).*

Step 2:

Cut out the individual months/pages *(you might want to get an adult to help you with the scissors).*

Step 3:

Glue or tape each Calendar Tab into the 'month' space on each page.

Step 4:

Using one of the pages as a stencil, place on the flattened cereal box, draw around it and then cut it out so that you the have a blank card.

Step 5:

Completely unfold the CD case so that it forms a stand. Then insert all the pages into the CD inlay tabs, with the blank card at the back for support.

POLICE LINE DO NOT CROSS
POLICE LINE DO NOT CROSS
POLICE LINE DO NOT CROSS

ARSEY COPS

PC FROSTY

JANUARY

POLICE LINE DO NOT CROSS
POLICE LINE DO NOT CROSS
POLICE LINE DO NOT CROSS

ARSEY COPS

PCs GRIZZLY & SURLY

FEBRUARY

183

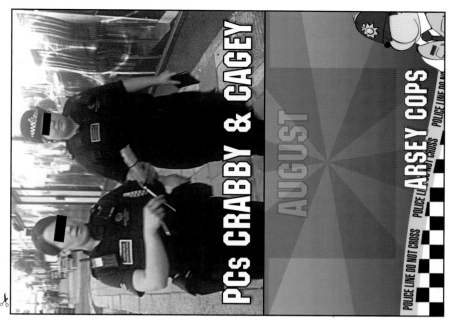

PCs CRABBY & CAGEY

AUGUST

ARSEY COPS

POLICE LINE DO NOT CROSS

PC STROPPY

JULY

ARSEY COPS

POLICE LINE DO NOT CROSS

185

PC PEEVEY

SEPTEMBER

POLICE LINE DO NOT CROSS

ARSEY COPS

PC STUFFY

OCTOBER

POLICE LINE DO NOT CROSS

ARSEY COPS

187

CREDITS

Susan McNicholas
Greg Matthews
Tracey Moberly
Tine Selby
Mike McCarthy
Warren Lakin
Hannah MacDonald and everyone at September Publishing

PD
Rikki Blue
Bex Colwell
Jeff Jenkins
Guy Taylor
Noel Douglas
Shamik Dutta
Richard Stein
Rosa Curling
Simon Natas
Tiernan Douieb
Chris Coltrane
Sam Riddle
Vanessa Furey
Dan Mudford
Grainne Maguire
Angela Barnes
Curzonistas
Veronica Pasteur
Dave O'Carroll
Bipasha Ahmed
Bill Bailey
Billy Bragg
Ben Van der Velde
Nicky Branch

Emma Callander
Theatre Uncut
Bridget Christie
Josie Long
Robin Ince
Dawn Purvis
Alliance for Choice
Jonny & the Baptists
Lesley Hart
Phil Nichol
Rob Hoon
John McManus
Lindis Percy and her lovely chum
Rick Burgess
Dr Simon Duffy
The Centre for Welfare Reform
Nick Dilworth
Jane Bence
Wayne Blackburn
New Approach
Black Triangle Campaign
DPAC (Disabled People Against Cuts)
Francesca Martinez
WOWpetition
Mental Health Resistance Network

Glasgow Against ATOS
Liz Crow
Atos Stories
Atos Miracles
Pat's Petition
Carer Watch
Derbyshire Unemployed
Workers' Centre
Anne-Marie Comber
Archibald Foundation
False Economy
Unite Community
Susan Calman
Dayna Alexander
Joe Lycett
Stephen K. Amos
Zoe Lyons
BECTU
Unite
GMB
Blacklist Dave
Peekay
Jason N. Parkinson
Jess Hurd
Jules Mattsson
Adrian Arbib
David Hoffman
NUJ
UCATT
Sarah Kavanagh
Free Tibet
London Charity Softball League

Millennium Gallery, Sheffield
Rosie, Chris, Ben and the crew
The Leadmill
Danny Clarke
Tori Hope
Glenn Estes
Lucie Walton
Hannah Rose
Kayleigh Wilson
Patricia Rodgers
Mel Maine
War on Want
John Hilary
Adina Claire
Tim Hunt, *Ethical Consumer*
Michelle Stanistreet, NUJ
Hilary Jones, Lush
Nat
Jonnie Marbles
Red Pepper for loan of barge pole
Tony and Dexter
Police Spies Out of Our Lives
Living Wage Foundation
Jonny Walker
Elis James
John O'Farrell
Nick Revel
Martin Pople
Juliet Slide
Phil Stebbing
Matt Tapley
Danny Shine

Everyone who played, put stickers on things, suggested definitions, waved banners, jumped around in cinemas, Tescos and parks. SALUT!

Special thanks to Jenny, Charlie and Izzy

THE RULES OF MINOR DISSENT

1. 100 Acts of Minor Dissent to be committed in one year, from **14 May 2013** to **13 May 2014**.

2. Verification of the Acts committed will be conducted at a live performance in Sheffield on **15 May 2014**, where each and every Act will be counted and confirmed.

3. Should 100 Acts be committed, the materials used in creating the Acts will form the basis for a free week-long art exhibition at the Millennium Gallery in Sheffield.

4. Should 100 Acts fail to be committed, a forfeit shall be levied. **That forfeit shall be the donation of £1,000 to UKIP.**

700043005288